Anxiety Disorders

Psychological Disorders

Anxiety Disorders

Sucheta Connolly
David Simpson
Cynthia Petty

Series Editor
Christine Collins, Ph.D.

Foreword by
Pat Levitt, Ph.D.
Vanderbilt Kennedy
Center for Research
on Human Development

CHELSEA HOUSE
PUBLISHERS
An imprint of Infobase Publishing

Anxiety Disorders

Chelsea House
An imprint of Infobase Publishing
132 West 31st Street
New York NY 10001

Library of Congress Cataloging-in-Publication Data

Connolly, Sucheta.
  Anxiety disorders / Connolly, Sucheta, Cynthia L. Petty, David A. Simpson.
      p. cm.
  Includes bibliographical references and index.
  ISBN 0-7910-8543-0 (hardcover)
  1. Panic disorders—Juvenile literature. 2. Post-traumatic stress disorder—Juvenile literature. 3. Phobias—Juvenile literature. 4. Anxiety—Juvenile literature. I. Petty, Cynthia L. II. Simpson, David A. III. Title.
  RC535.C66 2006
  616.85'22—dc22   2006004996

Series and cover design by Keith Trego

Printed in the United States of America

Bang EJB 10 9 8 7 6 5 4 3 2 1

This book is printed on acid-free paper.

All links and web addresses were checked and verified to be correct at the time of publication. Because of the dynamic nature of the web, some addresses and links may have changed since publication and may no longer be valid.

Table of Contents

Foreword

Pat Levitt, Ph.D.
Vanderbilt Kennedy Center
for Research
on Human Development

Think of the most complicated aspect of our universe, and then multiply that by infinity! Even the most enthusiastic of mathematicians and physicists acknowledge that the brain is by far the most challenging entity to understand. By design, the human brain is made up of billions of cells called neurons, which use chemical neurotransmitters to communicate with each other through connections called synapses. Each brain cell has about 2,000 synapses. Connections between neurons are not formed in a random fashion, but rather, are organized into a type of architecture that is far more complex than any of today's supercomputers. And, not only is the brain's connective architecture more complex than any computer, its connections are capable of *changing* to improve the way a circuit functions. For example, the way we learn new information involves changes in circuits that actually improve performance. Yet some change can also result in a disruption of connections, like changes that occur in disorders such as drug addiction, depression, schizophrenia, and epilepsy, or even changes that can increase a person's risk of suicide.

Genes and the environment are powerful forces in building the brain during development and ensuring normal brain functioning, but they can also be the root causes of psychological and neurological disorders when things go awry. The way in which brain architecture is built before birth and in childhood will determine how well the brain functions when we are adults, and even how susceptible we are to such diseases as depression, anxiety, or attention disorders, which can severely disturb brain function. In a sense, then, understanding how the brain is built can lead us to a clearer picture of the ways in which our brain works, how we can improve its functioning, and what we can do to repair it when diseases strike.

Brain architecture reflects the highly specialized jobs that are performed by human beings, such as seeing, hearing, feeling, smelling, and moving. Different brain areas are specialized to control specific functions. Each specialized area must communicate well with other areas for the brain to accomplish even more complex tasks, like controlling body physiology—our patterns of sleep, for example, or even our eating habits, both of which can become disrupted if brain development or function is disturbed in some way. The brain controls our feelings, fears, and emotions; our ability to learn and store new information; and how well we recall old information. The brain does all this, and more, by building, during development, the circuits that control these functions, much like a hard-wired computer. Even small abnormalities that occur during early brain development through gene mutations, viral infection, or fetal exposure to alcohol can increase the risk of developing a wide range of psychological disorders later in life.

Those who study the relationship between brain architecture and function, and the diseases that affect this bond, are neuroscientists. Those who study and treat the disorders that are caused by changes in brain architecture and chemistry are psychiatrists, psychologists, and psychiatric social workers and nurses. Over the last 50 years, we have learned quite a lot about how brain architecture and chemistry work and how genetics contribute to brain structure and function. Genes are very important in controlling the initial phases of building the brain. In fact, almost every gene in the human genome is needed to build the brain. This process of brain development actually starts prior to birth, with almost all the neurons we will ever have in our brain produced by mid-gestation. The assembly of the architecture, in the form of intricate circuits, begins by this time, and by birth, we have the basic organization laid out. But the work is not yet complete, because billions of connections form over a remarkably long period of time, extending through puberty. The brain of a child is being built and modified on a daily basis, even during sleep.

While there are thousands of chemical building blocks, such as proteins, lipids, and carbohydrates, that are used, much like bricks and mortar, to put the architecture together, the highly detailed connectivity that emerges during childhood depends greatly upon experiences and our environment. In building a house, we use specific blueprints to assemble the basic structures, like a foundation, walls, floors, and ceilings. The brain is assembled similarly. Plumbing and electricity, like the basic circuitry of the brain, are put in place early in the building process. But for all of this early work, there is another very important phase of development, which is termed experience-dependent development. During the first three years of life, our brains actually form far more connections than we will ever need, almost 40% more! Why would this occur? Well, in fact, the early circuits form in this way so that we can use experience to mold our brain architecture to best suit the functions that we are likely to need for the rest of our lives.

Experience is not just important for the circuits that control our senses. A young child who experiences toxic stress, like physical abuse, will have his or her brain architecture changed in regions that will result in poorer control of emotions and feelings as an adult. Experience is powerful. When we repeatedly practice on the piano or shoot a basketball hundreds of times daily, we are using experience to model our brain connections to function at their finest. Some will achieve better results than others, perhaps because the initial phases of circuit-building provided a better base, just like the architecture of houses may differ in terms of their functionality. We are working to understand the brain structure and function that result from the powerful combination of genes building the initial architecture and a child's experience adding the all-important detailed touches. We also know that, like an old home, the architecture can break down. The aging process can be particularly hard on the ability of brain circuits to function at their best because positive change comes less readily as we get older. Synapses may be lost and brain chemistry can change over time. The difficulties in understanding how architecture gets built are paralleled by the complexities of what happens to that architecture as we grow older. Dementia associated with brain deterioration as a complication of Alzheimer's disease, or memory loss associated with aging or alcoholism are active avenues of research in the neuroscience community.

There is truth, both for development and in aging, in the old adage "use it or lose it." Neuroscientists are pursuing the idea that brain architecture and chemistry can be modified well beyond childhood. If we understand the mechanisms that make it easy for a young, healthy brain to learn or repair itself following an accident, perhaps we can use those same tools to optimize the functioning of aging brains. We already know many ways in which we can improve the functioning of the aging or injured brain. For example, for an individual who has suffered a stroke that has caused structural damage to brain architecture, physical exercise can be quite powerful in helping to reorganize circuits so that they function better, even in an elderly individual. And you know that when you exercise and sleep regularly, you just feel better. Your brain chemistry and architecture are functioning at their best. Another example of ways we can improve nervous system function are the drugs that are used to treat mental illnesses. These drugs are designed to change brain chemistry so that the neurotransmitters used for communication between brain cells can function more normally. These same types of drugs, however, when taken in excess or abused, can actually damage brain chemistry and change brain architecture so that it functions more poorly.

As you read the series Psychological Disorders, the images of altered brain organization and chemistry will come to mind in thinking about complex diseases such as schizophrenia or drug addiction. There is nothing more fascinating and important to understand for the well-being of humans. But also keep in mind that as neuroscientists, we are on a mission to comprehend human nature, the way we perceive the world, how we recognize color, why we smile when thinking about the Thanksgiving turkey, the emotion of experiencing our first kiss, or how we can remember the winner of the 1953 World Series. If you are interested in people, and the world in which we live, you are a neuroscientist, too.

Pat Levitt, Ph.D.
Director, Vanderbilt Kennedy Center
for Research on Human Development
Vanderbilt University
Nashville, Tennessee

Authors' Note

Anxiety disorders as a group are the most common form of mental illness among children and adolescents, but they are often underreported and undertreated. This book has been written to help young people who would like to learn more about the development, diagnosis, and treatment of the major anxiety disorders. It is our hope that this information may help youth appreciate risk factors that contribute to the development of anxiety disorders, recognize anxiety disorders in themselves or others, and help identify and understand the effective treatments for anxiety disorders. This book focuses on current evidence from scientific studies along with the clinical experience of the authors.

The authors would like to express their gratitude to the children and teenagers from the Pediatric Stress and Anxiety Disorders Clinic at the University of Illinois at Chicago who contributed to this book by sharing their own experiences with anxiety disorders. It is the courage and determination of the children and families we work with that inspired us to write this book. We are thankful for the opportunity to see many of them conquer their fears and appreciate all that we learn from them every day.

The major anxiety disorders covered in this book include generalized anxiety disorder (GAD), separation anxiety disorder (SAD), social phobia, specific phobia, panic disorder, obsessive-compulsive disorder (OCD), and post-traumatic stress disorder (PTSD). This book focuses primarily on the presentation of anxiety disorders in children and teenagers but also discusses how these problems may persist into adulthood. First, normal fears and worries are discussed along with the development of anxiety disorders. Then evaluation and treatment for anxiety disorders is reviewed as a group of disorders. Finally, each anxiety disorder is considered separately, with detailed examples of how it presents in youth and how treatment is modified for each anxiety disorder.

Development of Anxiety Disorders

1

NORMAL FEARS AND WORRIES VERSUS ANXIETY DISORDERS

Fear and worry are common in children, teenagers, and adults and are a normal part of development. Normal fears and shyness need to be separated from anxiety disorders that interfere with regular functioning in a person's life in school, work, friendships, or family. For example, anxiety disorders can make it difficult to take tests at school, participate in sports or parties, spend time with friends, or even relax and have fun.

Infants experience normal fears of loud noises, being startled or dropped, and later a fear of being held by strangers. Toddlers and preschoolers have normal fears of monsters and imaginary creatures, darkness, and anxiety over separation from their parents. Children of elementary school age experience normal worries about illnesses, injury, and natural disasters (such as tornadoes). Older children and teenagers have normal worries and fears related to academic performance, what peers and classmates think about them, and health issues.

Fears during childhood are normal but may become a problem if they increase or interfere with daily life. For example, a little difficulty separating from parents is common on the first day of preschool or kindergarten. Separation anxiety disorder (SAD), however, can make it difficult to remain at school even at an older age due to unreasonable fears that something bad

Figure 1.1 People who suffer from anxiety disorders often have trouble handling everyday tasks. For young people, anxiety can make it hard to take tests and perform well in school.

may happen to parents while away from home or that the parents may never come back to pick up their child. Children with SAD show excessive fear and distress with separation from home or their parents. Generalized anxiety disorder (GAD) is characterized by chronic and uncontrollable worry that is present nearly every day and in all kinds of situations. Social phobia results in excessive fear in social or performance situations with worries of doing something embarrassing or dumb in these situations. Specific phobia is excessive fear of a particular object or situation that may include avoidance of it. Panic disorder involves repeated anxiety attacks that occur without any trigger. Children with agoraphobia avoid places where they fear they will be unable to get help or escape if necessary. All of these anxiety disorders make it hard to function in day-to-day situations such as school, family life, and with friends.

ANXIETY DISORDER STATISTICS

Anxiety disorders are very common worldwide in both children and adults. **Prevalence** rates for children or teenagers having at least one anxiety disorder range from 6% to 20%. If anxiety disorders are diagnosed carefully and only counted if they are interfering in the child's life, the rate drops to 6% to 10%. Girls are somewhat more likely than boys to report an anxiety disorder, especially specific phobia, panic disorder, agoraphobia, and separation anxiety disorder. Some anxiety disorders start at an earlier age, including separation anxiety disorder, generalized anxiety disorder, and specific phobia. Panic disorder often starts in the mid-teen years.

The long-term course of anxiety disorders that start in childhood is still not clear. However, it seems that these disorders are less likely than experts once thought to go away on their own. When one anxiety disorder gets better in a child, another anxiety disorder may appear at that time or later. Also, the more severe the anxiety disorder, the more likely it is to continue into later years.[1] Anxiety disorders during the teenage years have been shown to increase the risk for anxiety and depression in adulthood.[2] When anxiety disorders persist over time, their impact on daily life continues to grow.

IMPACT ON SOCIAL, ACADEMIC, AND EMOTIONAL FUNCTIONING

Anxiety disorders interfere with the normal social development of children and teenagers. Social phobia makes it difficult to socialize with others and may keep teenagers from dating, establishing friendships, attending parties and dances, or participating in clubs. Children with separation anxiety disorder may remain dependent on their parents due to difficulty leaving them to be alone with friends as they get older. Social and emotional problems may include poor coping and problem-solving skills, low self-esteem, a tendency to underestimate one's own strengths, and a tendency to see things in a negative way.[3] When faced with a move to a new community, a teenager with anxiety disorder may assume he will not be as smart as his new classmates, will look different, and will never make good friends. Instead of introducing himself and getting to know his classmates, he may try to be as invisible as he can so he does not upset anybody.

Anxiety disorders may interfere with the concentration needed to complete schoolwork. Perfectionistic worries and performance fears of GAD may make it difficult to take tests, especially timed tests. One study found that first graders with high levels of anxiety were at risk for continued anxiety symptoms and lower academic achievement in reading and math when they became fifth graders.[4] A study in New Zealand followed teenagers with anxiety disorders who were not in treatment into adulthood and found that they had high rates of anxiety, depression, drug dependence, and educational underachievement as young adults.[5] There is growing evidence that anxiety disorders can have a negative impact on school functioning and academic success.

RISK AND PROTECTIVE FACTORS

The development of anxiety disorders in children and adolescents involves a complex interaction between **risk** and **protective factors**.[6] Risk factors increase the probability of developing a psychological problem. Protective factors strengthen psychological health and counteract the impact of risk factors.

Biological risk factors include genetics and temperament. Scientists commonly use studies that compare twins raised in

Figure 1.2 Although scientists believe there are physical causes, such as problems with brain chemistry, that lead to anxiety disorders, there are also environmental risk factors. Parents who don't handle stress well, for example, may teach their children inappropriate coping skills.

the same and different families to examine the impact and interplay of genetic and environmental influence in the development of a variety of psychiatric disorders. Several twin studies show that both genes and the environment in which children are raised contribute to the development of anxiety disorders in youth. When parents have anxiety disorders, their children have an increased risk for anxiety disorders and the children may experience more severe forms of anxiety disorders. **Behavioral inhibition** is a temperamental style in very young children that increases the risk for anxiety disorders in childhood and social phobia in teenagers.[7] Behavioral inhibition is characterized by shyness, caution, emotional restraint, and a tendency to avoid new situations. **Temperament** consists of individual differences in behavioral style or emotional reactivity that are present in early life and often persist over time.

Environmental risk factors in the development of anxiety disorders in youth include parent-child interactions and parental anxiety. Anxious parents can model fearful and anxious responses to everyday situations. They may unknowingly encourage anxious coping skills and avoidance in their children, in their desire to keep the child safe from harm or upset.[8] Parents who are overprotective, overcontrolling, or overly critical may prevent their children from developing independence and self-confidence, and may also increase the risk for anxiety disorders in their children. Children who do not develop a stable attachment or healthy bond with their parents early in life may also be at increased risk for anxiety disorders. Moving from one foster home to another, the death or absence of a stable parent early in life, or living with a single parent who remains severely depressed are all situations that may make it difficult for a child to establish a stable attachment or healthy bond with a parent.

Healthy coping skills have been identified as protective factors in childhood anxiety disorders, and learning coping skills is an important goal in the treatment of anxiety disorders.[9] Anxiety tends to lead to **avoidant coping**, where a child copes by avoiding the feared object or situation, experiences fearful thoughts about bad things that might happen, and does not have an opportunity to see that it is possible to face the fear successfully. Developing active coping strategies, distraction strategies, and problem-focused coping have been especially helpful for young people with anxiety disorders.[10] Social support also seems to be important in how children learn to cope with stressors and may be a protective factor as well. More research is needed to look further at both of these and other possible protective factors. Scientists are working on identifying children who are at risk for anxiety disorders earlier and developing interventions that can reduce the impact of these disorders on the lives of children and teenagers.

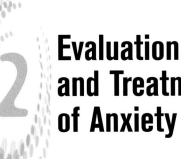

2 Evaluation and Treatment of Anxiety Disorders

EVALUATION FOR ANXIETY DISORDERS

Everyone worries once in a while. Normal fears and worries need to be separated from anxiety disorders in the process of diagnosing anxiety disorders in children and teenagers. It is important to consider the impact of stresses and traumas that have affected the child or family and may have started the anxiety or worsened the anxiety in the patient's life. An evaluation by a health professional looks for medical causes for the anxiety **symptoms**. For example, thyroid disease, consuming too much caffeine, migraine headaches, and asthma may all lead to anxiety-like symptoms. Sometimes, taking medications, such as cold medicines or asthma treatments, can also bring on "anxiety" symptoms, like feeling jumpy and restless or having trouble falling asleep. Finding a health professional who has training and experience with children and adolescents is also important.

Children and teenagers with anxiety disorders experience more fear and worry than other children their age, but they may not realize that what they feel is unreasonable or excessive. The anxiety may be expressed through crying, irritability, and angry outbursts when they have to face situations or objects they fear. They often have physical symptoms such as stomachaches or headaches that are related to the anxiety.

Figure 2.1 Anxiety disorders may cause the patient to feel fear, worry, and excitement all at once. These feelings can be very overwhelming and confusing. This abstract drawing of anxiety was done by a young patient named Bridget.

Anxiety disorders often happen at the same time as other anxiety disorders or other **co-occurring** psychiatric disorders such as **major depression, attention-deficit/hyperactivity disorder** (**ADHD**), or drug and alcohol abuse. It is important to determine all the different disorders that a person has to come up with the best plan for treatment. This can be difficult when one disorder is severe or many disorders cause the same symptoms. For example, ADHD, depression, and anxiety disorders can all lead to restlessness or difficulty concentrating at school. Sometimes, when one disorder is treated, the presence of another is easier to notice.

During the evaluation, the family and affected child or teenager may be asked to complete questionnaires to help the

Figure 2.2 If someone is anxious, a good medical evaluation can help determine if there are medical causes for the problem or if the person is suffering from an anxiety disorder.

health professional make a proper diagnosis. Gathering information from the patient, parents, and teacher is very helpful. This can help identify how anxiety may be impacting the child or family in various ways. With GAD, the child may be most aware of how his or her perfectionism and self-doubt are interfering with school progress or friendships. With SAD, parents may notice how difficult it is for the child to go anywhere without them and how this affects the whole family. With social phobia, teachers are often aware of how the patient's anxiety affects relationships with peers and social activities. Getting information from all these people makes it more likely that anxiety disorders will be identified properly and effective treatment started.

Clinics that specialize in treating young people with anxiety disorders may read questions from the Anxiety Disorders Interview Schedule—Child Version (ADIS-C) as part of their evaluation to identify which anxiety disorder or disorders may be present. The doctor or therapist may also ask questions about factors such as the history of the patient's mother's pregnancy (to see if any complications during the pregnancy such as illnesses, medications, or substances may have contributed to the child's anxiety), general health, frequency of infections, family history of psychiatric and medical illnesses, social history,

My Anxiety

This was written by a young patient named Matt about his own experiences with anxiety, ADHD, and a learning disability.

I have had ADHD and anxiety for as long as I can remember and it wasn't always easy. At times, I had to go through panic attacks, freaking out, and being too afraid to enjoy myself. For example, whenever my family and I would go to a theme park, I was always scared to go on one of those big, fast, high, loopy metal roller coasters, but there are some exceptions. Also, when I was younger, I had trouble learning and making and keeping friends or even talking to friends or other people. I was held back once in first grade but after that I passed second through seventh grades easily. I'm in eighth grade this year. Besides my anxiety, I have to deal with a sometime annoyance, my little brother, who is very funny and athletic. I also have two loving parents, and my dog, Sparkles. Although ADHD and anxiety or any other disabilities may be tough you must remember don't you ever give up hope, because you are a survivor.

Figure 2.3 Danielle, a young patient, drew this picture to show how she felt before and after receiving treatment.

school functioning, coping skills, and stresses and traumas. It is important to help the doctor and therapist understand how much the anxiety disorder is affecting the child's life. All of this information is combined to develop a diagnosis and treatment plan to fit the child or teenager and family.

TREATMENT WITH PSYCHOTHERAPY

Treatment of young people with anxiety disorders may involve a number of interventions. These include educating the child and parents about anxiety, working with the school and medical doctor, psychotherapy, family therapy, and medications.

Treatment of children and teenagers with mild to moderate anxiety disorders often begins with **psychotherapy**, or "talk therapy." The psychotherapy with the most research to support it is **cognitive behavioral therapy** (**CBT**). In CBT, the patient learns coping skills and is given opportunities to practice these skills to develop a sense of control in everyday situations that may normally provoke anxiety.

There are five components of CBT for anxiety disorders in youth.[11] CBT starts with *psychoeducation*. This means that children and parents are taught to understand anxiety disorders and how CBT works. Then, s*omatic management skills training* teaches children how to monitor anxiety symptoms and use relaxation skills such as deep breathing, muscle relaxation, and thinking about relaxing images. *Cognitive restructuring* challenges negative thoughts and expectations that bad things will happen, and helps children learn to use positive self-talk. For example, a child with a phobia of dogs may see a dog and think, "The dog is going to attack me." He would practice positive self-talk such as "Most dogs are friendly" or "The dog is probably nice and nothing bad is going to happen." Children practice these strategies until they feel competent and comfortable. The **exposure** part of CBT is next. It brings the patient into anxiety-producing situations one small step at a time. A **fear hierarchy** rates situations and objects from least to most anxiety-producing. The exposures start with the least anxiety-producing things and the patient uses the coping skills learned earlier in CBT to bring anxiety down to a tolerable level in the presence of the things that cause anxiety. When a child gets control over an anxiety-producing

Figure 2.4 Psychotherapy is one of the most useful methods for treating people with anxiety disorders. One popular form of treatment is group therapy, in which the patient shares experiences with other anxiety sufferers, under the supervision of a qualified counselor.

situation, then the next item on the fear hierarchy is used. This gradual step-by-step process, called **systematic desensitization**, works up through the fear hierarchy until the highest level of anxiety is mastered. Exposures often start with **imaginal exposure** in which the patient just imagines the feared situation or object, or looks at pictures, movies, or models of the object. Live or **in-vivo exposure** with the real-life situation is done once imaginal exposures feel comfortable and the patient is using coping skills successfully. *Relapse prevention plans* use booster sessions to check in after improvement and keep the patient stable. The therapist works with parents and the school as well as the patient to keep anxiety low.

Because participating in CBT exposures forces the patient to go through a temporary increase in anxiety as he or she works toward conquering fear, positive rewards are used as encouragement. With a **positive reinforcement** plan, children receive rewards for practicing their anxiety management skills and trying exposures, as well as rewards for eventually achieving success with exposures. The CBT program is personalized by the therapist to suit the specific needs of an individual child or family.

The best studied and most widely used CBT program is the Coping Cat program, which uses the five components of CBT in an entertaining workbook format geared toward children 7–14 years old. The Coping Cat program, developed by Philip Kendall of Temple University, needs to be modified by a therapist for use with children who are younger or older. This CBT program can be used for individual treatment or in a group setting.

CBT is not effective for all children and teenagers with anxiety disorders. Also, CBT for anxiety disorders may not be available yet throughout the United States because many mental health professionals have not been trained to use it. Other types of psychotherapy, including therapy with the patient, parent-child interventions, and family interventions, are often used along with CBT. More studies are needed to compare CBT to other types of therapies for anxiety disorders.

PARENT-CHILD AND FAMILY INTERVENTIONS

Research suggests that parents and families may play a role in the development and maintenance of childhood anxiety disorders. Therefore, parents and families are routinely involved in the treatment of children and adolescents with anxiety disorders. In CBT, parents learn anxiety reduction strategies and work with the therapist as a "coach" to assist the child in practicing and mastering new coping skills. As part of the therapy process, parents may also model healthy coping skills in situations that make the child anxious. Parental involvement in treatment may be most important when a parent is anxious or has an anxiety disorder. The therapist may work with the family to improve the parent-child relationship and communication skills, strengthen family problem-solving, reduce anxiety in a parent, or assist parents to encourage healthy coping skills in their child and increase the child's independent functioning.

Family therapy looks at patterns of behavior in the family rather than focusing on an individual. Family therapy with young people who suffer from anxiety may examine parental criticism, control, or emotional overinvolvement. Changing patterns of behavior between the parent and child can help a child build confidence in the new coping skills learned in psychotherapy.

SCHOOL INTERVENTIONS

Often, anxiety disorders interfere with a young person's functioning at school, and a plan is developed with the school's cooperation to assist the student with these struggles as the anxiety disorder is treated. Parents, teachers, and the affected student often meet to discuss problems caused by anxiety and to develop classroom strategies that can help the child become more successful at school. For test-taking anxiety, it may be helpful to give the child untimed tests in a quiet environment. If anxiety makes it difficult to finish homework, the length of assignments may be modified. It is often helpful to have a school staff member or team to assist the child with anxiety management strategies when fears worsen or become overwhelming at school. The treatment plan used in the school setting may change as the student's anxiety improves. It is helpful for the young person with anxiety to receive positive feedback from teachers and parents for using coping strategies to remain at school even when his or her anxiety may be worse in the school environment than elsewhere.

MEDICATIONS

There are several circumstances in which a combination of medication and psychotherapy is used to treat young people with anxiety disorders. First, if an anxiety disorder is severe, it may not be possible for the patient to take part in psychotherapy that involves exposures and facing fears. Adding medication can ease anxiety levels enough to allow for more effective treatment with talk therapy. Second, in many situations, something needs to be done quickly to reduce severe interference from the anxiety while psychotherapy is started. In other cases, a co-occurring disorder such as ADHD or depression may be present along with the anxiety and may need to be treated with medication. Medications can assist in situations in which a child's anxiety has only partly improved with psychotherapy.[12]

Serotonin Reuptake Inhibitors

According to current research in youth with anxiety disorders, the most effective medications are a group of antidepressants known as the selective serotonin reuptake inhibitors (SSRIs). Examples of SSRIs include fluoxetine (Prozac®), sertraline (Zoloft®), and fluvoxamine (Luvox®), to name just a few. Anxiety disorders may result from lower-than-normal levels of serotonin in the brain. Serotonin is an important **neurotransmitter**—a special chemical signal that allows communication between brain cells (neurons). SSRIs increase the levels of serotonin in the central nervous system (the brain and spinal cord). In adults, SSRIs are also considered highly effective for anxiety disorders.

Before starting any medication, it is important to have a thorough psychiatric evaluation to rule out other disorders, such as **bipolar disorder**, that may be affected by SSRIs or other medications. SSRIs are also preferred for young people with panic disorder and have shown some good results, but no controlled studies in youth are available. SSRIs generally have few side effects, which are usually mild and short-term, including stomach upset, diarrhea, headaches, restlessness, and trouble sleeping. Less common side effects include agitation or disinhibition that leads to uncharacteristic defiance of authority, acting without thinking through things, and getting upset easily. SSRIs can take several weeks to show an effect (and may take up to several months to begin to work completely).

Doctors follow patients closely for side effects and suicidal thoughts when any antidepressants, including SSRIs, are started and when dosing changes are being made. The risks and benefits of different medications are discussed by doctors with a child and family.

Other Medications

Other medications may be needed when several SSRIs have been tried and proven ineffective, or are only partially effective in relieving the patient's anxiety. Additional medications may also be necessary when co-occurring disorders such as ADHD make treatment more complicated.

Some antidepressants work on the norepinephrine (another neurotransmitter) receptor in the brain as well as the serotonin receptor and increase the amounts of neurotransmitters such as norepinephrine and serotonin available in the brain. These medications include venlafaxine (Effexor®) and tricyclic antidepressants (TCAs). Doctors may use venlafaxine as an alternative or along with the SSRIs when needed to better control a range of anxiety symptoms. The TCAs are used less often than SSRIs because they require blood levels to be closely monitored and have possible serious side effects related to the heart. TCAs may be used alone or to boost the effects of SSRIs, with monitoring for side effects such as dry mouth, lightheadedness, or changes in blood pressure and pulse.

Benzodiazepines are a class of drugs that have tranquilizing, sleep-inducing, and muscle-relaxing properties. Examples of benzodiazepines are clonazepam (Klonopin®), lorazepam (Ativan®), and alprazolam (Xanax®). Benzodiazepines are well studied in adults and are used as an alternative to SSRIs or buspirone for GAD or along with SSRIs or other antidepressants for panic disorder. In children and teenagers, more studies are needed to see just how effective benzodiazepines are. Benzodiazepines are prescribed by doctors for short-term use in youth to quickly reduce severe anxiety enough to make participation in exposures possible, and while SSRIs are taking effect. For young people with chronic and severe anxiety who do not respond well enough to other medications or therapies alone, benzodiazepines may be helpful. However, they need to be used with caution for several reasons: 1) the risk of developing dependence on the medication when it is used daily for longer than several months, and difficulty stopping the medicine; 2) it is not recommended when drug or alcohol abuse is already a problem; and 3) it may cause side effects such as tiredness, difficulty with memory and concentration in school or at work, or disinhibition with irritability, so that the patient gets upset more easily.

Buspirone (BuSpar®) is a medication that reduces serotonergic activity in the central nervous system and may impact dopamine (another neurotransmitter). It has been shown to be an effective alternative to SSRIs and benzodiazepines for some adults with anxiety disorders, especially GAD, but there are no controlled studies in youth. It is not sedating like the benzodiazepines and does not have potential for addiction. The most common side effects in youth are lightheadedness, headache, and stomach upset.

3 Generalized Anxiety Disorder

As usual, Tim was having trouble sleeping on Sunday night. The same old worries kept running through his mind. He might forget to hand in his homework and upset his teacher. He might say the wrong thing to his friends and they might not like him anymore. His dad might lose his job. Every day his worries weighed him down like a backpack filled with bricks that he could never put down. It seemed like other kids could have fun most of the time rather than worrying so much. Tim suffers from generalized anxiety disorder.

STATISTICS

About 6% of the United States population suffers from generalized anxiety disorder (GAD). Studies in teenagers show that anywhere from under 1% to nearly 5% in the United States may suffer from GAD.[13] Most adults with GAD report that their anxiety started in childhood or as a teenager. They usually say they have been worrying all their life. Studies report no significant gender difference between boys and girls with GAD up to age 13, although GAD is more common in adult women than in men.[14] Children and teenagers with GAD often have other anxiety disorders, too, such as separation anxiety disorder and specific phobia.

CAUSES

The cause of GAD is not yet known. Recent studies have shown that there may be a genetic contribution to GAD in adults. More studies are needed to see whether children with parents who suffer from GAD are more likely to develop GAD themselves. As discussed in chapter 1, other factors such as shyness and inhibition from an early age, modeling of anxious coping by parents and others, stressors, and traumas also need to be considered in the development of anxiety disorders among children and teenagers. Medical illnesses that may mimic symptoms of anxiety disorders also need to be considered by a medical professional.

DIAGNOSIS

The current diagnosis of GAD is based on criteria in the *Diagnostic Statistical Manual of Mental Disorders* (DSM-IV). The DSM-IV lists criteria for making a diagnosis of all the different psychiatric illnesses in children and adults. According to the DSM-IV criteria children, teenagers, and adults with GAD experience worry that is unrealistic or excessive when compared with other people their own age. The worry they experience occurs often or all the time for at least six months. The worry and anxiety is not limited to a specific object or situation, but is present most of the time and relates to many areas, such as schoolwork and grades; performance on a job, in sports, or in music; physical appearance; health and safety of oneself and family; making friends or impressions on others; things that have happened in the past, like unpleasant conversations; or things that are going on in the world, such as war, crime, and weather. Anxiety can also come from feeling the need to be perfect, or perhaps the thought that negative things may happen in the future. People with GAD are unable to control or escape from their worry and anxiety.

Figure 3.1 Anxiety disorders don't take place in the mind alone. They also cause physical problems, including sleep disturbances, which can make it difficult to function in everyday life.

In addition to the worry, adults need to experience at least three, and children or teenagers at least one, physical problems as a result of their anxiety. These physical problems can include sleep disturbance, muscle tension, irritability, difficulty concentrating, restlessness, or fatigue. Anxiety, worry, or physical problems cause significant struggles in important aspects of life, such as socializing with friends, school or work performance, and relationships with family members. Anxiety can stop the child or teenager from doing things he or she would like to do. To qualify as GAD, the anxiety cannot be caused by a substance (e.g., a drug or medication) or a general medical condition (e.g., hyperthyroidism).

CASE STUDY

Tim Franklin was introduced at the beginning of this chapter. He was a 12-year-old boy who was a good student. He had many friends and was admired by his classmates for his athletic abilities. He had always been a bit of a worrier and a perfectionist. Last spring, his worries got worse. He never liked thunder, but now he could not sleep whenever there was a storm. He began to watch the weather channel regularly. About the same time, he saw a scary movie with some older friends and could not get some of the frightening images out of his mind. He was constantly worried that bad things would happen to him or his family.

He developed headaches and frequently went to the nurse's office at school. A full medical examination by his doctor did not reveal any specific medical cause for his headaches, but his doctor was concerned about how tense and restless Tim looked.

Over a few months, Tim found that his worries about storms were making it difficult for him to spend time outside with friends. He also continued to develop more fears about crime in his neighborhood and felt safer staying at home. His fears were not based on any evidence; he lived in a very safe area. His fears also kept him from participating in sports. When he did see friends, Tim was grouchy and could not relax and enjoy himself. His friends knew he had always been a worrywart, but they were concerned about these changes and mentioned their feelings to him. He began to have doubts about what his friends thought of him.

At school, Tim had difficulty concentrating in his classes because his mind was filled with doubts and worries. He studied as hard for tests as he always did, but then felt like his brain was "melting down" when the test started. He continued to get mostly As and Bs, but he feared that his grades were slipping and felt he needed to study more. This isolated him even further from his friends. He routinely turned down invitations to games and parties because he felt he needed to prepare for school. His teachers commented that he looked very tired and

Figure 3.2 Generalized anxiety disorder (GAD) affects people in many different ways. Some people may cry while others may get irritable or angry. A young patient named Catherine drew this picture to represent her own struggle with generalized anxiety disorder.

didn't seem to be having fun with other students the way he did before. He developed stomachaches that seemed to get worse on Sunday night before the school week started. He missed several days of school because of his stomachaches and headaches. This made things worse because it made him feel like he was getting further behind in his schoolwork.

At home, Tim was unusually grouchy and argumentative. When he was anxious or overwhelmed, he looked restless and worked himself up until he was screaming and crying about minor matters. As his sleep problems grew worse, he often sought reassurance from his parents at night, which made it hard for his parents to get enough rest. His parents were also concerned that Tim seemed unhappy and had begun to blame himself for other people's problems.

Tim and his family sought help from Tim's pediatrician, Dr. Burt. Dr. Burt had already ruled out other medical problems with blood tests. He also asked Tim if he drank soda with caffeine or took any cold or allergy medicines that might be contributing to his difficulty sleeping and restlessness. Dr. Burt then referred Tim to a psychiatrist for a full evaluation. Tim was not eager to see a "shrink" and worried about what his friends would say. However, he knew his worries were messing up his life. He agreed to go to the psychiatrist but said he did not want any of his friends, other relatives, or teachers to know. Only he and his parents would know. Dr. Burt and his parents agreed.

Tim completed an evaluation with Dr. Smith, a psychiatrist who specialized in working with children and adolescents. Dr. Smith gathered information from Tim, his parents, and Dr. Burt. She asked Tim to let her get information from teachers about how Tim was doing at school, but Tim refused. Tim revealed during his first interview with Dr. Smith that he felt overwhelmed by his worries and just wanted them to stop. Lately, Tim felt that if this worrying continued, then it seemed like life might not be worth living anymore. Tim did not want to hurt himself and had never tried to hurt himself in the past. At the visit, Tim's mother shared her own struggles with anxiety, which had been going on since she was in grade school. Tim was surprised to learn about this, but it made sense since his mother often seemed to be stressed out about her work and keeping up her schedule. Tim's mother was on a medication that helped ease her anxiety, and she had also received talk therapy when she was in college, which also helped her. Mrs. Franklin noted that Tim always had some difficulty falling asleep, but it had become worse over the past year. She saw some of the same problems in him that she had experienced when she was younger. However, she was not properly diagnosed until she was an adult. Mrs. Franklin hoped that getting Tim the help he needed now could prevent him from going through some of the things she had faced.

Tim was diagnosed with GAD. Depression was also considered because of his problems with sleep, irritability and mood, and decreased interest in doing things he usually enjoyed with friends. Dr. Smith explained that she would like to monitor his depression and suicidal thoughts closely to see if they improved as his anxiety got better. Because of the severity of Tim's anxiety and his mother's positive response to medication, Dr. Smith, Tim, and his parents decided to try both medication and talk therapy for his problem.

Tim had some trouble sleeping the first few nights on the medication and felt a little more restlessness, but these problems went away in the first few weeks on the medication. The medication helped Tim worry less, and he was able to engage successfully in cognitive-behavioral therapy on a weekly basis for several months.

Tim's parents participated in the CBT, too, and learned about how his physical symptoms, tension, irritability, and other struggles were all connected with his GAD. They also learned relaxation skills and coping skills along with Tim. Now his parents could provide him with rewards for practicing his relaxation skills, positive self-talk, and trying to expose himself to anxiety-provoking situations. They did their best to resist coming to his rescue too quickly when he appeared to be in distress and helped him develop a sense of self-competence in managing things on his own. Dr. Smith

Figure 3.3 Relaxation techniques, such as yoga and meditation, can calm the mind and body and help to reduce anxiety.

instructed them not to participate in his reassurance-seeking behavior. Instead, Tim benefited from his parents' praise and their encouragement to make some of his own decisions.

As Tim learned more about GAD and felt comfortable with his treatment, he agreed to involve his school in the process. Over a four-month period, he experienced significant improvement in his GAD symptoms. In six months, he felt back to his old self. He was better able to make decisions for himself and relied less on fears of negative evaluations by other people. He found he could relax and enjoy activities and successes without constantly thinking ahead to his next goal. He continued to have some occasional struggles in certain situations, but he felt confident in his ability to cope with these on a day-to-day basis. He was enjoying his friends and school again. He had monthly visits with Dr. Smith to monitor his medication and coping skills, but eventually he needed to see her only every few months. Once he was stable and doing well for a full year, his doctor said they could consider reducing his medication slowly to see if he could manage his anxiety without it, using only the coping skills he had learned through CBT.

Certain symptoms of GAD, such as feelings of tension, apprehension, reassurance-seeking, irritability, negative self-image, and physical symptoms, may occur more often in children and teenagers than in adults.[15] Physical symptoms commonly include stomachaches or headaches that may require frequent trips to the school nurse or doctor's visits that do not reveal other medical causes.

People with GAD, like Tim, are often described as "worry-warts." The desire to do everything perfectly is also common with GAD. Children and teenagers who have GAD often need excessive reassurance from others about their worries and find it hard to reassure themselves. Because of their self-doubt and distress, they find it hard to make decisions. Dealing with conflicts or upset feelings can be painful for people with GAD. They may try to please others to avoid conflicts. People with GAD may experience the world as a place that is not safe, where bad things can happen for no reason. Often, there is a tendency to focus on negative remarks and events rather than positive ones. It is difficult for people with GAD to appreciate their own strengths or successes, as a result of their tendency to be overly critical of themselves.

The distress that people with GAD experience may not be apparent to others, and they often suffer in silence. GAD in children and teenagers may lead to depression, as in Tim's case, or substance abuse over time if it is not identified and treated. This is true of other anxiety disorders as well.

Catherine's Story

This was written by a patient with anxiety.

It didn't come as a surprise to me when I was first formally diagnosed with anxiety (a few different types). I had been having issues with sleeping, school, slumber parties, etc. You get the picture. I had been to a few counselors before, but it wasn't helping. After a lot of researching, my mom found a clinic that specialized in child and teen anxiety. I went and took a "formal diagnostic test," which consisted of a lot of questions. It was worth it, though. I was diagnosed with generalized anxiety disorder, as well as a few other types. After learning a lot of exercises, we decided to put me on medicine. I took the medicine to help get me calm enough in stressful situations, so that I could use the techniques and exercises I'd learned. Since then, I have had great success with my anxiety. Occasionally I will hit a bump in the road, but I've managed, and now am feeling better than ever! One of the many things that I was struggling with was my weekly allergy shot. I would do anything I could to try to get out of them. If my mom was able to get me there, then I would be very upset, crying, screaming—the whole nine yards. Now, I can go without worrying about it three days ahead of time, or anything!

No matter how severe your anxiety is, you can get through it! The best advice I can give you is as follows:

- Even if something [suggested as treatment] seems pointless or stupid, it can't hurt to try it.
- Find some good books or other resources that you can use to improve your knowledge!
- If you are going to see a counselor or psychiatrist take the time to find someone that you like and can trust!

The best thing I can tell you is to never give up!

INTERVENTIONS

Parental involvement in the CBT treatment process is encouraged whenever appropriate, but it is not required. CBT usually involves parents so they can better understand their child or teenager's anxiety and assist the patient in using new coping skills. Parents also learn how to provide positive rewards for their child's efforts in the treatment process.

Through CBT, young people with GAD become aware of their physical responses to anxiety and can use this awareness to use the relaxation strategies they learn. This is especially helpful when they have severe physical complaints like stomachaches and headaches. CBT also teaches how to identify the anxious thoughts and negative things that people say to themselves. Perfectionistic children and teenagers with GAD benefit from developing more realistic expectations and substituting positive self-talk for negative self-talk. An important goal of CBT is to teach the patient problem-solving skills and coping strategies that help him or her feel more confident when faced with things that usually make him or her feel worried or overwhelmed. CBT also encourages anxious people to reward themselves for their efforts in facing their fears and overcoming some of their worries.

In addition to CBT, other types of therapy have also been useful for people with GAD, including working with the family, depending on the unique struggles of the child, teenager, or family. Significant losses, stresses, and traumas are often shared by all family members and need to be addressed. Also, if a parent has an anxiety disorder, then it is important that the parent be treated as well as the child. The therapist or doctor can help provide parents with guidance on how to decrease the impact of their own anxiety disorder on their parenting style. Parents play an important role in helping young people with GAD decrease avoidance of anxiety-provoking situations and in encouraging appropriate autonomy and self-reliance.

Interventions at school that involve teachers, counselors, and school nurses can be very helpful, especially when the GAD is directly impacting school performance or attendance. The child or teenager will need to discuss with parents and doctors or therapists what information will be important to share with people at school. It will be necessary for the school staff to understand what GAD is and what its impact is on the student, and to learn how to provide positive rewards for the student's efforts at tackling the anxiety. Since physical complaints are common with GAD, it is useful to develop a plan for how to help the student stay at school and use coping skills to manage the anxiety rather than to just send the student home. The student with GAD may also experience anxiety during exams and worry about grades, and may strive to hand in perfect assignments. It may be difficult for the GAD patient to cope with academic struggles or anything less than meeting his or her own high expectations. Cooperation among the parents, therapist or doctor, student, and school staff can dramatically help the student succeed in reducing the impact of the anxiety disorder in the school.

Medications may also be used in some cases of GAD. The medications that have shown the most success in controlled studies of anxiety disorders in children and adolescents, including GAD, are the antidepressants that are **selective serotonin reuptake inhibitors** (**SSRIs**).

In Tim's case, an SSRI medication helped reduce his anxiety and depressive symptoms so that he could participate fully in CBT and make a successful recovery from his GAD. Dr. Smith worked with Tim, his family, and his school to help Tim address the impact of GAD in various parts of his life. Some psychiatrists can provide all of these interventions, while others will provide medications and have a separate therapist provide the talk therapy.

Separation Anxiety Disorder

Do you remember being scared to be away from your parents?
You might have been upset if you were separated from them, or
if you knew they were going to the store without you. Or maybe
you refused to go to school, to sleepovers, or to parties because
you were afraid that you would not see your parents again. If so,
you may have suffered from separation anxiety disorder, a condition that usually affects how children or adolescents react to
being away from a parent or their home.

STATISTICS

Separation anxiety disorder (**SAD**) is an anxiety disorder that
affects approximately 4% of children.[16] The hallmark feature of
SAD is overwhelming anxiety and fear concerning separation
from people to whom the child is attached, usually parents. The
child may experience intense fear and anxiety when he or she is
away from home. It is important to remember that separation
anxiety is normal for children between the ages of seven months
and six years. SAD becomes more diagnosable when an older
child or adolescent experiences intense anxiety and fear when
separated from parents or while away from home.

CAUSES

There are many triggers that can lead to the development of
SAD. These include significant stressful life events such as the

Figure 4.1 It is normal for very young children like this one to become anxious when they have to be separated from their parents. In older children, however, an excessive fear of being away from a parent or guardian may be considered an anxiety disorder.

loss of a loved one or pet, a childhood illness, the illness of a relative, or a change in school or family structure.[17] SAD and other anxiety disorders do not occur solely as the result of some event or environmental circumstance. Anxiety disorders of all kinds tend to occur more often in some families and less in others, so children of anxiety sufferers are more likely to have anxiety than are the children of parents who do not have an anxiety disorder. There is good evidence that anxiety disorders like depression, heart disease, or high cholesterol run in families. It is important to keep in mind the fact that the age at which a child experiences a loss or a possible loss has an influence on whether or not he or she will experience SAD, as well as the severity and intensity of SAD symptoms, should they occur.[18]

There are many examples of environmental influences on anxiety levels. Some parents lack appropriate coping mechanisms when they are anxious. Their children are then exposed to coping mechanisms that may prove ineffective when the child is faced with stress or anxiety. As a result, the child or adolescent may become even more anxious when separated from the parent. Parents may also not understand the developmental milestones that their children go through. For example, it is normal for youngsters to explore their environments, but parents may become overprotective of their children and continually caution them, eventually making the child more anxious about his or her own activities. A child may also develop SAD if he or she perceives rejection from a parent, like if the child feels a parent is indifferent to his or her behavior.

Because SAD is characterized by the fear of losing a loved one, usually a parent, children or adolescents who have experienced the loss or threat of the loss of a parent have an increased risk for developing SAD. Other environmental disruptions have also been linked to the development of SAD. These include changes in the family, such as divorce, or starting a new school. When children and adolescents go through these changes, they can become vulnerable to SAD and show many behavioral disruptions, such as clinging to parents or refusing to go to school.

DIAGNOSIS

For SAD to be diagnosed, the patient must experience "developmentally inappropriate and excessive anxiety concerning separation from home or from those to whom the individual is attached."[19] The patient must have three or more of a list of symptoms for at least four weeks, including recurrent excessive distress when the person anticipates separation from home or from those to whom he or she is attached; persistent and excessive worry about losing loved ones or about possible harm befalling them; and persistent and excessive worry that a negative event, such as getting lost or being kidnapped, will lead to separation from a major attachment figure. Additional symptoms include an ongoing reluctance or refusal to go to school or elsewhere because of the fear of separation, being overly fearful or reluctant to be alone or without major attachment figures at home, or without significant adults in other settings; persistent reluctance or refusal to go to sleep without being near a major attachment figure, or to sleep away from home; repeated nightmares involving the theme of separation; and complaints of physical problems, such as headaches, stomachaches, nausea, or vomiting when separation from major attachment figures occurs or is anticipated.

To qualify as SAD, the symptoms must occur before the age of 18 and must cause significant distress or impairment in social settings, academic settings, or other facets of life.

CASE STUDY

Marc was a seven-year-old second-grader at the local elementary school. He completed all his work on time and did well on tests. His favorite subject was spelling. As the school year progressed, he began to experience "butterflies" in his stomach every morning before going to school. He told his mother that he was afraid something would happen to her while he was away. His mother reassured him that nothing would happen and that she would be waiting for him at home after school. Marc told his mother he had the same feeling in his stomach and same thoughts every morning for about two weeks. At this time, Marc's teacher told his mother that Marc would often mention that he was worried about whether his mother was safe at home. Marc also began to complain that he was going to "be sick" and would ask to see the school nurse. The nurse would find nothing wrong with Marc and he would return to his classroom.

One of Marc's friends at school had a birthday party one weekend. Marc was invited, but he was afraid to go, since he would have to be away from his mother during the party.

SCHOOL REFUSAL BEHAVIOR

School refusal behavior has many causes, including anxiety disorders and depression. Some children and adolescents experience anxiety that is so intense that they choose not to attend school. For example, children who have SAD are afraid to be away from home or their parents for fear that something terrible may happen either to themselves or their parents. Therefore, they think it is safer to stay at home and make sure that they do not get separated from their parents. When children have social phobia, they are too afraid to be in school and around other students for fear they will do something embarrassing or will be humiliated. Again, they feel safer at home and avoid going to school. School refusal behavior has a negative impact on treatment for both SAD and social phobia, since the affected child or adolescent is avoiding the anxiety-producing stimuli and is not exposed to situations that will help him or her learn to overcome the fear.

Although he was afraid that something would happen to his mother, he decided to go anyway. During the party, Marc told his friend's mother that he had a stomachache and wanted to go home. Marc's mother came and picked him up from the party. When he returned home, Marc no longer complained of a stomachache.

After several weeks, Marc's symptoms began to get more intense. He was no longer able to sleep alone in his bed at night. He would often run out of his classroom to try to leave school to be with his mother. Marc was never able to make it out of school, and his mother was called to come pick him up on several occasions. This led Marc to start refusing to go to school because he was so afraid that something terrible would happen to his mother.

Marc's parents decided that something needed to be done about their son's distress and fear. He was taken to a nearby clinic for an evaluation and was diagnosed with separation anxiety disorder. Marc and his family were in therapy for several months. Over the course of treatment, Marc and his family learned ways to cope with distressing thoughts and anxiety. The family and school helped Marc return to school on a permanent basis by setting up reachable goals to help him stay in his class. Marc's mother went to school regularly at first and less frequently over time. This helped Marc become reacquainted with the school surroundings while his mother was present. Marc would then spend longer spans of time at school without his mother. As a result, he had less anxiety about being away from her. In addition, Marc was able to spend time at friends' homes and even attend sleepovers. Eventually, Marc was able to develop friendships and succeed at school.

Figure 4.2 Sometimes, young people with separation anxiety disorder are so unwilling to leave their parents that they miss out on the social activities that most kids their age enjoy.

ADDITIONAL INFORMATION

When children or adolescents with SAD are separated from their parents, they experience an overwhelming fear that they will not be able to see their parents again as a result of some catastrophe.[20] A person suffering from SAD may report fearful thoughts that something will happen to a loved one or that he or she will be kidnapped and never see certain loved ones again. These fears of loss lead affected children to exhibit various behaviors that help keep them close to loved ones or to their homes. These behaviors vary in form and intensity and often depend on the child's age.

For example, 5- to 8-year-old children might begin to worry that something bad might happen to a parent or to themselves and that they will ultimately be separated from their loved ones. Children in this younger age group may begin to follow their parents around the house. An older child, between the ages of 9 and 12, might begin to complain about physical symptoms, such as an upset stomach or headache, on school days. Children in this age group may also show excessive distress and will withdraw and look sad when separated from a parent. Adolescents between the ages of 13 and 16 will also complain of physical symptoms, may be reluctant to leave home, and may avoid school to try to stay near a parent. Adolescents often deny that they are anxious when separated from a parent, but they may limit their participation in independent activities when their family is not present.[21]

In addition to the above characteristics, other behaviors may be present that can help children or adolescents minimize their level of distress. These vary in intensity and duration. Patients with SAD often want their parents to be available by telephone or otherwise easily accessible while they are away from home. Children and adolescents with SAD may also refuse to attend sleepovers or other activities that force them to be away from their parents or away from home for several hours at a time. Those with more severe cases of SAD may engage in school refusal behaviors or be unwilling to sleep alone in their beds. In the most serious cases, children and adolescents with SAD will come up with elaborate stories or excuses to explain why they need to be with their parents at all times.[22] Avoidance behaviors often cause patients to miss developmentally appropriate activities. They may, for example, limit their involvement in sports or other group activities in the community, at school, or at church, which might cause problems in social development and the establishment of friendships.

Evidence suggests that children and adolescents who suffer from SAD have a greater risk of developing social phobia and depression as they get older, if they do not receive adequate treatment for SAD. Females in particular are at greater risk for developing panic disorder and agoraphobia.

INTERVENTION

The goal of treatment is to expose the patient to situations where he or she is away from parents. Often, the patient's parents and school take an active role in this part of the treatment. There are times when it is difficult for the parents to see their child as an independent person. In some cases, parents can work with the clinician to learn appropriate ways of coping to help their child overcome SAD.

In some cases, treatment for SAD may also include medications. The medications that have shown the most success in controlled studies of anxiety disorders in children and adolescents, including SAD, are the antidepressants that are selective serotonin reuptake inhibitors (SSRIs). Medication may be considered when the SAD is severe and can help reduce the anxiety symptoms so that the patient can participate fully in CBT.

Social Phobia

Have you ever refrained from participating in class because you thought others would think what you said was stupid? Have you stayed home from a dance or party because you thought you might do something embarrassing? If so, you may be suffering from a common condition called **social phobia** (or social anxiety disorder).

STATISTICS

Social phobia is an anxiety disorder that affects approximately 3% to 4% of children and adolescents.[23] Individuals who experience it are fearful that they will get into situations that will cause them embarrassment and/or humiliation. They also fear being scrutinized by others. Their fear is so great that they will avoid social situations, which leads them to experience even more anxiety when they have to be in social situations, leading to even more avoidance.

CAUSES

As with all anxiety disorders, children and adolescents are at greater risk for developing social phobia when they have parents with an anxiety disorder. In addition to its heritability, social phobia has a significant relationship to the temperament of the affected person. People who would be described as "shy" or "quiet" by parents and peers are at a greater risk. Shy children and adolescents may not answer questions in class, invite friends over after school, or accept invitations to others' homes. They will look for ways to avoid situations that cause them anxiety and try to avoid being the center of attention.[24] This behavior can interfere with the person's ability to overcome social phobia.

SELECTIVE MUTISM

Many children with selective mutism also have social phobia. Some scientists believe selective mutism may be a type of social phobia that develops early in childhood. A child with selective mutism does not speak, read aloud, or sing in certain social situations (such as at school) even though he or she will speak in other situations (such as at home with family). It may be possible for the child to whisper or communicate nonverbally through writing or by pointing to things in some situations with certain friends or teachers. Affected children are often filled with fear when they try to speak outside a "safe zone" of people or places that feels comfortable to them. For example, a child may feel comfortable talking and laughing with parents, siblings, and close friends at home but find it difficult to speak with family when they are at the grocery store, laugh with friends at school, or talk with anyone they do not know. Parents, siblings, friends, and teachers may try to help by speaking for a child with selective mutism, but this can often make it harder for a child to overcome the fear and speak for him- or herself. The treatment of selective mutism involves the child, parents, and teachers working together and often includes cognitive-behavioral therapy, and in severe cases, medication.

Children and adolescents with social phobia have fewer and less-effective coping skills than other people when they experience anxiety in social situations. When people have limited coping abilities, they may feel less confident when they go into anxiety-producing situations. This is evident when children and adolescents begin to think about the physical symptoms that go along with their social phobia. For instance, as they begin to worry that others may be aware of their shaky hands or flushed complexion, they have trouble realizing that there are alternatives to their negative thoughts related to these physical symptoms. This distorted cycle of thinking about their anxiety provides them with inappropriate coping skills in anxiety-producing situations. When social phobia sufferers avoid anxiety-producing social situations, they learn that this will reduce their anxiety. However, avoidance is not a suitable coping skill. It only limits the patient's ability to overcome social phobia in the long run.

Parents may not be aware of their child's struggles with social phobia. This is significant for many reasons. First, if parents are unaware of their child's problem with anxiety, they will not know that it is necessary to seek treatment. Second, if parents don't know that their child has social phobia and the child complains of physical symptoms because he or she wants to avoid school or other social situations, the parent may allow the child to stay at home. By allowing this, parents reinforce avoidance behaviors, which ultimately lead to continued struggles for the affected child or adolescent.

DIAGNOSIS

The DSM-IV suggests that social phobia in children and adolescents looks different from social phobia in adults. DSM-IV lists several symptoms that must be present for a diagnosis of social phobia in children and adolescents, and these differ from the criteria for the same diagnosis in adults. To have social phobia, a child needs to experience a marked and persistent fear of one or more social or performance situations in which he or she is exposed to unfamiliar people or to the possible scrutiny of others. The individual fears that he or she will act in a way (or show anxiety symptoms) that will cause him or her humiliation. Social relationships with familiar people such as close family and friends should be more comfortable. The anxiety must occur in peer settings, not just interactions with adults. Additionally, exposure to the feared social situation must almost invariably provoke anxiety, which may take the form of a panic attack. In young people, the anxiety may be expressed by crying, temper tantrums, freezing, or shrinking from social situations with unfamiliar people. The child recognizes that the fear is unreasonable, and that other children and adolescents do not have the same anxiety. The feared social or performance situations are avoided or are endured with intense anxiety or distress. The avoidance, anxious anticipation, or distress in the feared social or performance situations interferes significantly with the child's normal routine, academic functioning, and social activities or relationships, or the child experiences distress about having the phobia. To meet the criteria for social phobia for people under the age of 18, symptoms must be present for at least six months.

CASE STUDY

Robert was a 15-year-old male who was liked by his peers, did what his parents asked him to do, got good grades in school, and enjoyed building models. He was also extremely quiet in situations where many people were around. Crowded places such as school or family events could be packed with both people he did not know and people he did know; in all social situations, he was uncomfortable and spoke very little to people who were not in his immediate family or his close circle of friends.

Robert had many fears about being in social situations. He worried that people might see him do something that would embarrass him. His worry was becoming more frequent, and he dreaded going to school for fear that a teacher would call on him in class and he would have to speak in front of everyone. Robert was also worried that if he were called on in class, he would not know the answer and would be humiliated.

Anxiety about possible embarrassment in school quickly expanded to situations outside of school. Robert stopped calling his friends on the phone and was often quiet when he sat in the cafeteria at lunch. He stopped going to the mall with his friends and hanging out at their houses after school. Instead, he began to spend a lot of his free time in the library at school. He would often miss lunch because of the anxiety he felt in the school cafeteria. As time went on, Robert often found excuses not to go to school. He refused to attend any school sporting events, which upset him, because he enjoyed sports.

When his parents asked him if he wanted to go out to eat, Robert always hesitated before agreeing to go. He had to think of where they would eat and weigh the risks of an embarrassing situation occurring. When Robert first began to think about these risks, he would still go out with his parents. However, over time, he struggled more and more with his fear of being around people he did not know and tried to avoid going out whenever possible.

Over time, Robert began spending more time by himself or only with his immediate family. His parents saw this change in his behavior and asked him if there was anything wrong. Robert told his parents about his fear of being around other people, that he was afraid of doing something that would make him feel embarrassed. Robert's parents said they were glad he had shared his fears with them and promised to find a professional to help him deal with his problem.

Within a few weeks, Robert went to see a therapist who works with adolescents who struggle with social phobia. Robert and his therapist, along with his parents and school personnel, developed a plan to help Robert return to attending school regularly, increase his social involvement with his peers, and begin to spend more time with his parents outside their home. Robert also learned ways to cope with anxiety when he was at school, with friends, and with his extended family.

ADDITIONAL INFORMATION

A child or adolescent with social phobia will experience almost immediate anxiety in just about all social situations. This may lead them to avoid social events or endure them with extreme distress. Affected children and adolescents may also experience panic attacks if their anxiety gets too intense. Additional characteristics that may be present in people with social phobia include having few friends, avoiding group activities, and experiencing feelings of loneliness.

When children and adolescents who suffer from social phobia are in school, they struggle with reading out loud in class, being in the cafeteria, asking others for help, working in groups, and taking tests, to name just a few situations that produce anxiety. In Robert's case, he was often worried about being embarrassed. Because people with social phobia avoid these situations, they often fall behind others in their ability to develop meaningful relationships, fail to develop socially, and do not find employment when they are old enough to get a part-time job.

As mentioned earlier, some children and adolescents will experience panic symptoms when placed in social situations. Younger children will complain of stomach distress and illness

Figure 5.1 Young people who suffer from social phobia may have distorted views of what other people think of them, which can lead them to avoid school or other situations in which they believe their peers will judge or criticize them.

and parents may report that their children are "clingy." Children may avoid being the center of attention. Social phobia looks different in adolescents. Adolescents will become concerned about whether other people can tell that they are anxious. They will worry about whether they are blushing, sweating, shaking, or whether their voice cracks when they talk in front of others. This is similar to how adults experience social phobia. Once the adolescent begins to worry about whether others notice these external symptoms of social phobia, he or she begins to think, "Others can see I am anxious." This brings on more physical symptoms, leading to more thoughts about being anxious. This pattern can cause the adolescent to experience more and more anxiety. It is understandable then, that these adolescents begin to avoid participating in situations that provoke anxiety and become more isolated. However, isolation becomes an obstacle to overcoming social phobia. The more one avoids these situations, the more anxiety he or she will experience when social situations are unavoidable, which leads to more attempts at avoidance. In other words, what appears to be helping to reduce the anxiety only serves as a way to make the anxiety and social phobia continue.

Avoidance of social situations can lead to school refusal behavior. The child or adolescent with social phobia will try not

Kenyetta's Story

This was written by a patient with anxiety and depression.

When I first found out I had depression and anxiety, it really made me feel like there was something major wrong with me. I was scared. I had the fear that "I was going crazy." And I even had to have homeschooling because of the anxiety. My anxiety is social phobia, and it has caused problems for me such as going outside, finding friends. It has caused me to cry endlessly when I would have anxiety attacks along with my depression. I have even lost some friends that I have had. They thought I just did not want to be with them or play with them. But it wasn't that at all. It was that I was too scared to go out and see them. Now some of them understand what I was going through and that does make me feel a little bit better. To me, anxiety is a very painful experience. It is like you have a fear for absolutely no reason. It feels really weird to know that you are scared, but you don't know what for. And the depression just brings sadness, to go to school because of fears about being embarrassed in front of peers. They may avoid school if they are worried about body image and fear being judged when they have to change clothes for gym class. Adolescents may spend time in the library or school office to avoid being in situations that they believe will lead to embarrassment or humiliation.[25]

LONG-TERM RISKS

Adolescents who do not receive treatment for social phobia are at a greater risk of developing depression as adults and are also

has caused long crying periods, and makes me feel alone and lost.

There are people and things that have helped me through the struggle as I continue to recover. The people are my grandmother, my psychiatrist, and my wonderful counselor at school. Some of the strategies that have been helpful include relaxation skills such as taking deep breaths and visualizing my favorite color and favorite relaxing place. In my relaxing place, the sky is blue, the sun is out, the weather is warm, and I am lying on a blanket in the grass under a tree with my eyes closed, feeling the nice, cool breeze. I have been working on getting out more and riding the bus. At one time, I was afraid to even do those things. I am gaining my confidence and I am learning to assert myself. Medicine has helped me by reducing my anxiety and my depression. I have been in treatment for five years and each year is getting better for me. After I finish high school, I want to go to college and major in art. I want to be a cartoonist.

Figure 5.2 Young adults with social phobia often become isolated and avoid interaction with other teens. This kind of self-imposed isolation can make school a very lonely place.

at increased risk for alcohol or drug abuse.[26] Depression can develop as a result of the isolation brought on by avoiding social situations. Isolation leads to loneliness, which can turn into a decreased interest in participating in activities. This can lead people to feel hopeless or helpless. Substance use can begin in adolescents and adults with social phobia when they start to use alcohol or drugs to ease their anxiety when faced with anxiety-producing situations. For example, people may drink alcohol at a party to help them feel relaxed enough to enjoy these normally stressful situations. Thus, they begin to rely on the substance to ease their anxiety so that they can remain in the situation. Research into the academic impact of social phobia has shown that females with social phobia are at greater risk of dropping out of high school and that both males and females with social phobia are more likely to drop out of college.[27]

INTERVENTION

The cognitive-behavioral therapy (CBT) that would be used for a child or adolescent with social phobia involves exposing the patient to social situations. This is done in a specific way that allows the person to encounter situations that are less frightening first, and then move to more challenging situations. In addition to exposures, the child or adolescent with social phobia can benefit from learning social skills. This can be done individually or in a group setting with other people who have social phobia. Some group programs have found additional benefits when they add members who do not have social phobia to model healthy social skills.

Another component of treatment for social phobia may include medications. The medications that have shown the most success in controlled studies of anxiety disorders in children and adolescents, including SAD, are the antidepressants that are selective serotonin reuptake inhibitors (SSRIs). Medication may be considered when the social phobia is severe and can help reduce the anxiety symptoms so that the patient can tolerate the social exposures that are part of CBT.

6 Specific Phobia

Jessy was always scared of bees, but it did not really seem like such a big problem until it got in the way of doing things she wanted to do. It became hard for her to spend any time outside with her friends because she was afraid of getting stung. Just thinking about bees made her heart race, her palms get sweaty, and her stomach upset. She wondered how she was going to get through the summer. Jessy suffers from a specific phobia of bees.

STATISTICS

Specific phobia is an unreasonable fear of a particular object or situation that the person avoids or endures with great distress. Mild fear and worry are common in children and teenagers and are part of normal development. A specific fear can develop into a phobia if symptoms are strong enough to cause extreme distress, or if the fear leads to problems in functioning with friends, school, or family. There is some evidence that girls may have higher rates of specific phobia and are viewed by others as more fearful than boys, but the reasons for these gender differences need to be studied further.[28] The fear and disability associated with specific phobia of mild to moderate severity may improve without treatment in some young people, but it may persist over time for others. Severe phobias may persist for one to five years in children, and it should not be assumed that the phobias will

Figure 6.1 Claustrophobia—the fear of being in an enclosed space, such as an elevator—is one common form of specific phobia.

go away on their own. Adults with phobias often report that their phobias started in childhood.[29] Specific phobias often happen at the same time as other anxiety disorders and it is difficult to tell how common they are apart from these conditions.

CAUSES

A range of biological and environmental factors contributes to the development and maintenance of anxiety disorders in children. For specific phobia, these factors include genetic influences toward fearfulness, temperament, anxiety disorders in parents, family members who encourage anxious or **avoidant coping** (avoiding things that cause fear or worry), and negative life experiences that may contribute to a specific fear.

The Phobia: A Poem by Charlotte, a Patient With Anxiety

The image,
That vision,
That stays frozen in your mind,
Captured,
A prisoner,
Of the penetrating stare,
Of your mind's eye,
Unable to tear your sight away.
You are transfixed by an image,
That constantly haunts your vision,
Until it finally seeps away,
But at every mention,
Every glance,
It reappears,
Vivid,
And somehow felt,
At the tips of your fingers:
The disgusting,
Stomach turning,
Shiver-making,
Feel,
And in your ears,
The unheard sliminess,
And crackling
That on anything else
Would be fine.
But connecting,
It terrifies,
Makes twitches,
And abnormal fidgets,
Overcomes logic,
In a tidal wave,
Drowning a desperate,
Unheard
Scream.

DIAGNOSIS OF SPECIFIC PHOBIA

It is very important to be sure that the unreasonable fear or avoidance is truly specific to a certain object or situation to make a diagnosis of specific phobia. The fear is not present in the patient all the time, as with GAD. The current diagnosis of specific phobia in the United States is based on criteria in the DSM-IV. Children, teenagers, and adults with specific phobia struggle with marked and repeated fear that is unreasonable when a feared object or situation is present or when they anticipate being exposed to it. The fear results in a sudden anxiety response that may be a panic attack. Children may express their anxiety by crying, tantrums, freezing, or clinging, and may not be aware that their fear is excessive. A fear is considered a phobia if it interferes with the person's normal routine, work, school, friendships, or family life, or if the person experiences marked distress about having the phobia. In children and adolescents, the fear needs to last at least six months to be considered a specific phobia. Young people should be given a diagnosis of specific phobia only after other anxiety disorders have been ruled out. However, other disorders, such as separation anxiety disorder, are commonly present along with specific phobia.

There are five subtypes of specific phobia. **Animal type** (fear of animals or insects) often begins in childhood. **Natural environment type** (fear of storms, heights, water, or darkness) also often starts in childhood. **Blood-injection type** (fear of getting shots, having blood tests, or seeing blood on a cut) runs in families and may result in fainting. **Situational type** (fear of transportation by cars, buses, planes; enclosed places such as elevators, tunnels; or bridges) tends to start in childhood or in the mid-twenties. **Other type** includes fear of doctors or dentists, vomiting, loud noises, costumed characters, choking, and contracting an illness or disease.

Jessy was a 14-year-old freshman in high school who was introduced earlier with her fear of bees. She was a shy baby who tended to cling to her parents in her early years. Over time, she developed a number of friendships and enjoyed being with other children.

From a young age, Jessy was always somewhat afraid of bees and wasps. She tended to keep her distance from them and jumped when they buzzed by her ear. Jessy's mother was scared of bugs when she was a little girl, too, but grew out of her fears. Jessy's father experienced anxiety attacks before he had to give a speech at a social function or a presentation at work. Neither of Jessy's parents had ever sought help for their anxiety.

One night, when Jessy was in fourth grade, she was playing in the yard and stirred up a wasp nest she did not know was there. She was stung once before she was able to get away. She was upset for hours and her parents could not calm her down. Medicines helped reduce the swelling and redness at the place she was stung, and she was fortunately not allergic to the sting. However, Jessy found it difficult to spend any time in the yard or park that summer without experiencing fears that she might get stung again. Her friends were frustrated but agreed to stay indoors with her.

Jessy's fear of bees seemed to get a little bit worse each summer, and then improve in the winter. She missed a few field trips at school because of her fears and was not able to attend a summer band performance that took place outdoors. She tolerated the problem for several years, but she realized she needed help the summer before high school started. It was a long hot summer and the bees and wasps were everywhere. Jessy started to feel overwhelmed and could not leave the house during the hot part of the day due to her fears that she would be stung. She panicked whenever she saw a bee or wasp and had a rapid heartbeat, sweating, and trouble breathing. She knew there would be a freshman outdoor education trip in the early fall and she was worried that she would be too afraid to go. She did not want to start high school that way.

She decided to seek help from her pediatrician, Dr. Hill, and asked her parents to make an appointment. Dr. Hill did a complete physical examination and checked to make sure there was no other reason for Jessy's anxiety symptoms. Dr. Hill made a diagnosis of simple phobia—animal type (bees and wasps)—and recommended that Jessy see a therapist who worked with children and teenagers and had done a good job with another patient who was scared of dogs. Dr. Hill told Jessy and her family that she would be in touch with the therapist to see that Jessy was getting better. If she didn't improve, Dr. Hill would refer her to a child and adolescent psychiatrist for further evaluation and help. Jessy and her family agreed to this plan.

The therapist discussed the diagnosis of specific phobia. She reviewed with Jessy's family how cognitive-behavioral therapy (CBT) works and explained that Jessy would have to tolerate some anxiety during the treatment in order to get better, but this would help her overcome the anxiety eventually. They would contact Dr. Hill if medication was needed to help Jessy tolerate the CBT or if additional anxiety emerged. Jessy was highly motivated to succeed and wanted to start high school with reduced fears so that she would not have to miss any outdoor events.

Jessy went to therapy every week and was given homework assignments to complete between sessions to practice the coping skills she was learning. At first, she learned relaxation techniques, including deep "belly" breathing, relaxing her

Figure 6.2 Some people with phobias are able to relax themselves by visualizing places that make them calm and happy, like this beach drawn by a young girl named Manju with an anxiety disorder.

muscles, and visualizing relaxing colors and places. Jessy and her therapist created relaxing images in Jessy's mind and on paper that could help her when she felt overwhelmed. She also learned things she could tell herself in response to her negative thoughts when she did get scared.

Jessy learned to monitor her own anxiety and use her relaxation skills before it became too severe. She practiced bringing her Feelings Thermometer (see Figure 6.3) down to a 1 or 2 (a little bit worried) out of 8 (very worried) before she tackled anything that was a little bit more anxiety-provoking.

Jessy and her therapist started with exposures to bees through books, photos, movies, and plastic models. Then they moved on to images of bees that Jessy created in her

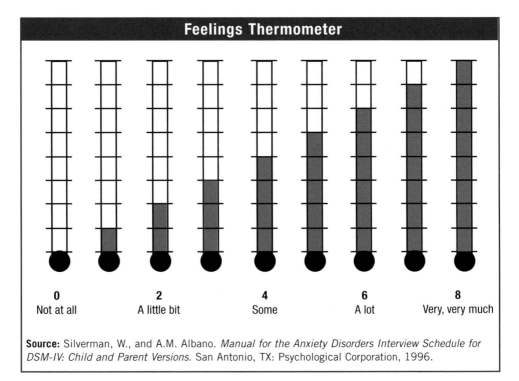

Feelings Thermometer

0	2	4	6	8
Not at all	A little bit	Some	A lot	Very, very much

Source: Silverman, W., and A.M. Albano. *Manual for the Anxiety Disorders Interview Schedule for DSM-IV: Child and Parent Versions.* San Antonio, TX: Psychological Corporation, 1996.

Figure 6.3 The Feelings Thermometer helps monitor how high or low anxiety is when the patient is exposed to different anxiety-producing objects or situations. When anxiety gets to be above the level of 2 or 3, the patient and therapist work to bring it down before moving on to another exercise.

mind or through drawings and other artwork. They moved from imaginal exposure to real-life exposure by taking trips outside the office. The therapist demonstrated healthy coping skills and approached bees and wasps in a calm fashion. She also discussed reasonable health and safety steps to take if Jessy did get stung. They spent more and more of their session time outside in the garden or a nearby field. They slowly moved closer and closer to the bees on flowers. Eventually, Jessy visited a beekeeper in the area with her family as part of her therapy homework. Jessy's confidence with bees and wasps carried over to other insects, too. Toward the end of therapy, Jessy received a bee sting, but based on what she had learned in treatment, she realized that she would survive this incident and would be all right if it happened again.

Jessy's parents learned relaxation strategies, too. They also provided **positive reinforcement**, giving Jessy rewards for her efforts to practice her relaxation techniques, do her best with her therapy homework, and eventually for succeeding in getting outside to the yard or the park. Jessy began to help with the family's flower and vegetable garden as part of her homework. Her friends were thrilled that she was willing to join them for outdoor concerts in the local park or to go on bike rides in the woods. Jessy was proud of her courage in fighting her fears and felt excited that she would be better prepared for the start of high school.

Jessy continued to meet with her therapist through the transition to high school, but needed therapy less often. Eventually, she saw her therapist only once a month to provide booster sessions and keep up her gains. She took a break over the winter and resumed booster sessions in the spring to be ready for any fears that might show up as the warm weather—and the bees—came back. Jessy did not require any medications for her anxiety.

INTERVENTIONS

It is important to consider the impact of stress or trauma on the development of a specific phobia. A diagnostic evaluation with a health professional who is familiar with treating children and adolescents is a good first step. This evaluation can consider medical conditions and other psychiatric disorders that may better account for the anxiety or may be happening with the specific phobia.

Figure 6.4 One way for people with specific phobias to overcome their fear is through gradual exposure to the feared object or situation. Here, a young woman is trying to overcome her fear of spiders through this method.

Among the treatments available for specific phobia, cognitive-behavioral therapies have received the most research support. Further studies are needed to evaluate the effectiveness of other types of treatment. A significant number of children may have only a partial response to CBT. Additional treatments, including other psychotherapies and medication, may become necessary when the specific phobia is severe or when CBT alone does not provide adequate relief.

The main focus of CBT in the treatment of specific phobia is gradual exposure. Children and teenagers are taught relaxation and verbal coping skills to fight off anticipatory fears or avoidance when anxiety-producing situations occur. They then engage in **systematic desensitization** with imagined or real-life exposures to the feared situation. **Modeling** is a technique in which a child learns to be less fearful by observing other people handling the feared objects and situations through films or videotapes (symbolic models) or in real life (live models) with a therapist, a parent, or other children. In **participant modeling,** a child is assisted by a parent or therapist to directly approach the feared object or situation.[30] Treatment often includes cognitive strategies to modify unrealistic fears that result in avoidance or distress. Exposure-based CBT treatment process requires raising the patient's anxiety to a distressing level. The therapist, parent, or both reinforce the patient's efforts to tolerate some discomfort and fight the fear with positive rewards. This helps shape good coping skills.

Medication may be considered when specific phobia is severe or if a good trial of CBT has only resulted in partial improvement. Medications that have shown the most success in controlled studies of anxiety disorders in children and adolescents, including specific phobia, are the antidepressants that are selective serotonin reuptake inhibitors (SSRIs). It may take SSRIs several weeks to show an effect, so benzodiazepines may be used in the short term to reduce anxiety symptoms quickly so the patient can participate in exposures.

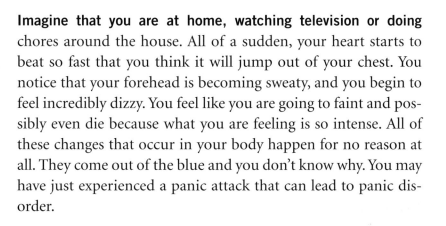

Panic Attacks and Panic Disorder

7

Imagine that you are at home, watching television or doing chores around the house. All of a sudden, your heart starts to beat so fast that you think it will jump out of your chest. You notice that your forehead is becoming sweaty, and you begin to feel incredibly dizzy. You feel like you are going to faint and possibly even die because what you are feeling is so intense. All of these changes that occur in your body happen for no reason at all. They come out of the blue and you don't know why. You may have just experienced a panic attack that can lead to panic disorder.

STATISTICS

Panic disorder is an anxiety disorder that affects approximately 0.3% to 1% of adolescents at any given time.[31] It usually affects more females than males during adolescence. Panic disorder looks different in children and adolescents of various ages compared to the same disorder in adults, which makes it difficult to diagnose panic disorder in children and adolescents. However, in recent years, more and more information about panic disorder has become available to clinicians who work with young people. It is important to keep in mind that panic attacks and panic disorder can occur along with other anxiety disorders. The information provided in this chapter will emphasize panic attacks and panic disorder in teenagers.

(*continued on page 66*)

Bridget's Story

This was written by a patient with anxiety.

When I was working at the pharmacy, a lady came up to the counter to pick up her medicine. She looked terrible. She appeared older than her age. She looked like she hadn't slept in days, with sunken eyes. She looked sad and overwhelmed. She said, "I am so worried when I have something stressful related to work the next day. I can't sleep because so many thoughts are running through my mind." I couldn't help but say to her "I feel for you." It was a reflection of myself and my own struggle with anxiety. She looked like she was in desperate need of advice. She said to me, "I can't believe that I am not the only one going through this," and she looked like she might cry. She was telling me that she has tried so many medications. I told her that there is something out there that will help you. I noticed she was talking fast, like I would when I was anxious. I told her that I hoped she would feel better. I told her that "I still have anxious times, but I want to tell you it does get better."

I have struggled with many anxiety disorders, including panic disorder and GAD, that really made it hard every day. In the past, in the classroom, I could not concentrate because of my fear that I looked anxious and people would notice my anxious behavior. I was worried they might ask questions such as "Are you okay?" and then I would feel even more nervous that I looked panicked. Rather than people asking if I'm okay, it is more helpful if I can let them know when I need help.

My fear of having panic attacks led me to avoid situations with people and certain places. Now I am driving, but in the past, I had panic attacks that prevented me from driving. Now my anxiety does not stop me from doing things with my friends. I feel I have control over my anxiety. I avoided going to the mall because there were so many people there. I would start hyperventilating and feeling dizzy when I saw too many people there. It got to the point that it was hard to walk. Walking out of the house started to make my heart start racing. Now I am on medications for my anxiety and have learned coping skills through cognitive behavioral therapy. What really helps me is to take deep breaths and say relaxing things to myself. At school, I was always at the nurse's office to escape my anxiety at school. Now if I need to step away, I go to the washroom and calm myself down on my own.

I used to worry about my school performance and thought I could not concentrate due to my anxious thoughts. I still worry that when a friend does not call for a few days, that the friend is upset at me, that I did or said something to offend him or her, even though I know this is not the case. I continue to worry about bad things happening to people I care about. For example, if I called my mom and she did not pick up her cell phone, I would worry, "Is she okay? Is she hurt?" I worry that having these thoughts might lead to bad things. My anxiety is better, but I still have work to do—like going to sleep at a decent hour or getting a blood test. I also continue to worry about getting all kinds of side effects on my medicine, but now I see that many of these thoughts are just my anxiety talking. At first, my worries about the side effects kept me from trying the medicine at all. I would also get confused about which physical feelings were related to my anxiety or were side effects.

When I graduated from high school, I was almost not going to attend my graduation. I was proud that I went despite my anxiety about the crowd and could hold my head high and feel good about succeeding despite my anxiety. My whole family and my friends have been so supportive through all this. I have shared my struggles with my close friends.

(*continued from page 63*)

CAUSES

There are many possible triggers or sources for panic attacks and panic disorder. Adolescents who are at risk for panic attacks include those who experience depressive symptoms, low self-esteem, or another anxiety disorder, or for whom a stressful situation had occurred shortly before the first panic attack.[32] A stressful event might be an increased workload in school, a change of school, or a negative drug experience. Disruptions in family life such as divorce, parental illness, or the death of a parent might also cause stress. Entering puberty is also a common trigger, particularly among females. Genetics and anxiety in an individual's family may lead to an increased risk for developing an anxiety disorder. Children and adolescents with the most worries were found to be the children of parents who where clinically anxious.[33]

Besides stressful events and family influence, the early temperament of children and adolescents can increase the risk of developing anxiety disorders. Young people who display a large range of emotions and variable behavior early on, as young as two years old, are at an increased risk of developing an anxiety disorder.[34] Children who may go on to develop an anxiety disorder were generally socially withdrawn, took longer to begin to speak, stayed close to their caretaker, were less active than their peers, and showed distressed behaviors. These children also exhibited muscle tension and a faster heart rate.

DIAGNOSIS

There is a difference between a panic attack and panic disorder. **Panic attacks** are repeated episodes in which a person experiences a collection of symptoms that are typical of panic disorder. At least four of a list of physical and cognitive symptoms are present and peak within 10 minutes. The symptoms of a panic attack include heart palpitations, a pounding heart, or accelerated heart rate; sweating, trembling, or shaking; sensations of shortness of breath or smothering; a feeling of choking; chest pain or discomfort; nausea or abdominal distress; feeling dizzy, unsteady, lightheaded, or faint; derealization (feelings of unreality) or depersonalization (being detached from oneself); fear of losing control or going crazy; fear of dying; paresthesias (numbness or tingling sensations); and chills or hot flashes. Having a panic attack alone does not mean that someone has panic disorder. Panic attacks can occur with any of the anxiety disorders. Panic attacks are common with specific phobia, social phobia, generalized anxiety disorder, and separation anxiety disorder in children and adolescents.

For a panic disorder to be diagnosed, the patient must experience repeated panic attacks that appear from out of the blue, along with at least one of the following criteria for at least one month: persistent concern about having additional attacks; worries about what the panic attack means or the consequences it will cause, such as losing control, having a heart attack, or "going crazy"; and a significant change in behavior related to the attacks.

It has been difficult to determine how often panic attacks and panic disorder occur in children and adolescents. This may be because some patients are not able to describe their symptoms clearly to a medical professional. For example, young children report a fear of being sick but may not report any specific physical symptoms that would lead the medical professional to realize the child is having panic attacks. Many children under the age of 12 have trouble describing a fear of dying, going crazy, or losing control, and instead simply report that they "feel sick." In recent years, medical professionals have worked to develop new ways to identify symptoms that will more accurately identify and diagnose panic attacks and/or panic disorder in children and adolescents. Medical professionals have begun to interpret young children's reports of being afraid of becoming ill or vomiting as a symptom of panic attacks. Adolescents begin to report fears of breathlessness, dizziness, rapid heart rate, and feelings of derealization and depersonalization.[35] Children and adolescents also report a fear of eating with a later fear of vomiting. When the medical professional hears the child or adolescent describe symptoms this way, he or she can ask the patient questions related to panic attack symptoms to find out if there are additional symptoms.

CASE STUDY

Nicole was a normal 12-year-old who had a supportive mother and did well in school. She enjoyed being with her friends, spending time with her mother, and playing on her school's basketball team. One day, Nicole was at a professional basketball game with her school basketball team. As she walked to her seat before the game, she began to feel dizzy and lightheaded, and had a pounding heart so intense that she thought it would jump out of her chest. In addition to these symptoms, Nicole felt like she was "going crazy" and did not know what was happening to her. As she experienced these symptoms, she began to have trouble breathing. Nicole immediately told one of the adults with her, who took her to the first-aid station at the arena. An ambulance was called and Nicole was taken to a nearby hospital for an evaluation. Within 25 minutes, Nicole's symptoms had gone away and she was doing well. Her mother met her at the hospital and took her home. Over the next 3 months, Nicole had about 11 more panic attacks and was taken to see a professional who worked with children and adolescents who have panic disorder.

Nicole's symptoms were similar to the symptoms experienced by other adolescents who have panic attacks, including rapid heart rate, abdominal distress, hot or cold flashes, shaking or jitteriness, dizziness, sweating, shortness of breath, feelings of unreality, and headaches.[36] At first, the panic attacks came from out of the blue. However, over time, they occurred when Nicole was in large crowds, such as at the cafeteria at school and at the mall. Before Nicole went for treatment, she had begun to avoid the school cafeteria, had reduced the amount of time she spent at the mall with friends, and had stopped going to basketball practices. Her avoidance was brought on by her fear of having a panic attack in these situations. These avoidance behaviors reduced Nicole's opportunities for socializing with peers, which led to feelings of isolation. Unlike other anxiety disorders, in panic disorder, the fear of symptoms of panic attacks remains the focus of the sufferer's fears, not necessarily a fear of particular places or situations.

Nicole spent five months in treatment and was able to overcome her fear of panic symptoms. This allowed her to spend more time with friends and helped her improve her performance in school as she no longer feared her symptoms.

ADDITIONAL INFORMATION

Adolescents diagnosed with panic disorder may avoid various situations, such as crowds or social events, for fear of having panic attacks. In general, they worry that it may be difficult to escape from these places or situations, or feel it will be embarrassing or hard to get help if they do begin to have a panic attack. The fear of going into places is called agoraphobia. The places most commonly avoided are situations with which the person is unfamiliar. These often include restaurants, crowds, elevators, parks, and stores. Some adolescents will refuse to attend school or engage in other activities that require interactions with their

Figure 7.1 Agoraphobia, the fear of being in places from which escape is difficult or help is unavailable, can occur when a person becomes isolated because of fears of suffering a panic attack. An agoraphobic person becomes almost a prisoner in his or her own home.

peers. Even though these interactions with peers may be in familiar settings, the adolescent continues to fear the possibility of another panic attack.[37] Avoiding situations in which a panic attack may occur interferes with a person's ability to overcome his or her anxiety and fear of symptoms.

INTERVENTION

The most effective way to overcome panic disorder is to experience the anxiety, enter the feared situations, and face the specific symptoms of a panic attack. CBT for panic disorder includes some unique strategies. Many young people who have panic attacks and panic disorder find a great deal of relief when they learn more about their condition, including information about why the physical symptoms appear. For example, hyperventilating or breathing fast can cause lightheadedness due to shorter breaths that lead to less oxygen entering the lungs and ultimately less oxygen available to the brain. Taking deep breaths can reverse this process and can help interrupt a developing panic attack. Once they have a better understanding of panic attacks, they learn better ways to handle their physical symptoms. They practice exercises that bring on the same physical symptoms that are associated with their panic attacks, such as dizziness, shortness of breath, and sweating. In this way, they are "exposed" to the physical and emotional aspects of their disorder. However, instead of feeling overwhelmed they learn to use coping strategies to calm themselves and go on with their activities. Through this type of exposure, called **interoceptive exposure**, patients become better equipped to take control over their symptoms.[38]

Treatment of panic disorder may include medications when the panic disorder is severe and can help reduce anxiety symptoms so that the patient can participate in CBT. The medications that have shown the most success in controlled studies of anxiety disorders in children and adolescents are the antidepressants that are selective serotonin reuptake inhibitors (SSRIs). In addition, benzodiazepines may also be used in the short term when a quick response is needed, until the SSRIs take effect.

Obsessive-Compulsive Disorder

Obsessive-compulsive disorder (OCD) has a prevalence of 0.3 to 1.0% in children and adolescents and a prevalence of 2.5% over a lifetime in adults.[39] OCD may affect as many as 1 in 100 children. OCD usually begins in adolescence or early adulthood but may begin in childhood. The average age at onset is earlier in males than in females: between 6 and 15 years for males and between ages 20 and 29 years for females. OCD usually begins gradually, but it can start suddenly in some cases. Most people get better and worse at various times over the course of their OCD, and their symptoms worsen when they are under stress, sick, or are not getting enough sleep.

OCD can be a disabling condition in which an individual experiences unwanted and disturbing thoughts, impulses, or images (obsessions) and/or engages in repetitive mental or behavioral acts (compulsions). Because people with this condition typically have severe anxiety, OCD is considered an anxiety disorder. To understand OCD, it is first necessary to know something about the nature of obsessions and compulsions.

Obsessions can be any unpleasant thought, scary image, unacceptable impulse, or object that causes fear or distress. These thoughts or images get stuck in the person's mind and replay over and over. In all cases, obsessions are involuntary and occur even though the person with OCD tries to resist them. Most people with this disorder understand that their obsessions are unrealistic or excessive, but feel unable to control them. Common obsessions include:

- Dirt, germs, contamination
- Doing something that might cause harm to others
- Making a mistake
- Thoughts perceived as evil or sinful
- Hostile or violent thoughts
- Sexual thoughts or impulses
- Thoughts about unacceptable behavior
- Disease or illness
- Things that are asymmetrical or imperfect

The anxiety and other feelings triggered by obsessions can be so distressing that children and adolescents with OCD come up with strategies to make themselves feel better. These strategies, called **compulsions**, or rituals, are attempts to relieve the distress caused by obsessions. For example, people who are afraid of dirt may wash their hands over and over again. A person who worries about causing harm to other people may spend hours checking to make sure the stove is turned off. Usually, compulsions are performed in a stereotyped, repetitive fashion.

Most people with OCD realize that their compulsions are unnecessary or counterproductive but feel unable to resist them. Because OCD sufferers are influenced by emotions more than logic, compulsions can be thought of as superstitious behavior. These are a few of the most common compulsions seen with OCD:

- Washing (e.g., hands, personal objects, house)
- Checking (e.g., locks, pilot lights, electrical outlets)
- Collecting or hoarding items (an inability to throw things away)

Figure 8.1 Obsessive-compulsive disorder is characterized by repeated rituals that help the affected person feel less anxious. One of the most common rituals is excessive handwashing, as seen here.

- Repeating certain movements over and over again
- Seeking reassurance
- Straightening or lining things up
- Placing items in a certain order or pattern

• Thinking about special numbers, images, thoughts, or designs in one's mind.

A diagnosis of OCD is made by using the DSM-IV diagnostic criteria for obsessive-compulsive disorder. A person must have either obsessions or compulsions, although many people have both. The obsessions must cause the person to feel very anxious, worried, or distressed. The person tries to ignore or stop the thoughts, impulses, or images, or to make them ineffective with some other thought or action. The person knows that the obsessions, impulses, or images are a product of his or her own mind (not felt to be coming from outside).

Compulsions are repetitive behaviors such as handwashing, checking things, or mental acts like praying, counting, chanting, or repeating words silently. The person feels driven to perform these actions in response to a worry or according to rules that must be rigidly applied. The behaviors or mental acts are used to decrease the worry or anxiety the person feels, but the behaviors are either not connected in a realistic way with what they are supposed to neutralize or are obviously excessive.

At some point during the course of OCD, the person notices that his or her obsessions or compulsions are unreasonable. Children, however, are often unable to recognize this. The obsessions or compulsions also cause a great deal of distress, are time-consuming (taking more than one hour per day), or significantly interfere with the person's normal routine at work or in school, or with usual social activities or relationships.

CASE STUDY

JF was a 10-year-old, straight-A student in the fourth grade who had been receiving counseling for two years. He was a perfectionist. His parents decided to bring him to an anxiety disorders clinic after they attended an educational conference sponsored by the Obsessive-Compulsive Foundation. They felt he had not improved since his counseling began. Instead, he continued to perform odd behaviors. His teacher had

Brian's Story

This was written by a patient with OCD.

MY WORST NIGHTMARE

Brian is a 10-year-old boy who is in 4th grade, but he has one more week until summer vacation. Last night, Brian thought, "What if mom and dad are going out?" He started getting worried and got up from his sleep to find his mom and dad to make sure they were home. This was the start of his OCD. They were home. Dad said, "You know we're here." Brian went back to his room. After sleeping for two hours, he got worried again about whether his mom and dad were there. Dad said, "Don't be silly Brian. We're here. Now go back to bed and please, please don't get up again. We are exhausted. It is not healthy to get out of bed because you need your sleep." Brian asked his mom, "Am I being cursed?" Mom said, "No, we just need to find out what's bothering you."

The next morning, Brian woke up and worried that he might have missed the bus for school. Then he checked the time and saw that he only had 45 minutes left to get ready for school. He was worrying and said to his mom, "Am I going to be late for school? Am I going to miss the bus?" Mom said, "Of course not, you still have 45 minutes, and that's plenty of time." Mom remembered that she had a friend who works at a nearby expressed concern and annoyance over his repeated questions in class. His parents reported that they were arguing with each other over how to deal with their son. JF's constant worry about being clean often made him late for school. He would get "stuck" in the shower, washing himself over and

juvenile research center, so she called and set up an appointment for after school. Brian said, "I'm not sick!" Mom said, "We need to figure out what's bothering you."

Brian went to school and, throughout the day, he was worrying. He became embarrassed because he kept asking his best friend and other people questions. He would ask: "Did I step on you? Was I in your way?" After school, Brian and his parents went to see Mom's friend, Mrs. O'Reilly. She asked Brian questions about how his worries have affected his life. "How many times do you get worried in a day? What percent of your life do you get worried?" Brian answered, "75%." She asked, "Do you ever get upset because you worry so much? Do you get sweaty or tired and things like that?" Brian answered all the questions that the doctor asked. After all questions were done, the doctor said, "You have OCD, which is obsessive-compulsive disorder." She said, "Think of OCD like a monster trying to bother you all the time. Let's try to fight the monster by thinking that you know it's okay or you didn't do anything bad. You can learn ways to use your thoughts to overpower the monster."

Brian and his parents went home and, every week, Brian would narrow down how many times he asked people questions. First, it was 20 times a day, then 15, then 10, and then 5. Finally, after a few months, he was able to fight the monster and free himself of OCD.

over until he felt clean enough. His father admitted that punishing JF did not help him change his behavior. His mother had to change her work schedule to help JF get to school every morning.

For the first four sessions of therapy, JF would not let his family out of his sight. He made very little eye contact and wrung his hands as his parents talked about their concerns. His mood was grouchy and he often said that he wanted to "get out of this dump!" He refused to sit in any of the office chairs because he feared they were "dirty," so he sat on his father's lap instead. During subsequent therapy sessions, he sat on a blanket that he brought with him from home. His hands were red and chapped from constant washing and he insisted that his mother carry wet wipes with her at all times. He looked tired and nervous. His mother tearfully reported that JF threw a tantrum and then stayed in the bathroom washing his hands with antibacterial soap for an hour after his younger sister (who had a cold) gave him a hug. He told his parents he did not want to catch her germs.

At school, JF would only drink his milk (which came in a sealed carton) because it was the only food that the cafeteria workers did not touch. According to his teacher, he asked the same questions over and over because he wasn't sure he understood the material correctly. He stayed up late doing his homework because he had to make sure he read every word on the page. He often read the same sentence 20 times before he felt that he really understood it. He asked his parents often if he was doing his math problems exactly right and was unable to start the next problem until he knew that the last one was done correctly. JF constantly worried about his parents and sister being safe and would anxiously question them about behaviors that he thought were risky. He had a series of several questions he asked all the people he

cared about: "Do you wear a seat belt? Do you have any tat-
toos? Do you have any body piercings? Do you smoke?" If his
parents were a few minutes late, he became tearful and pan-
icky, expressing his fear that they had been killed in a car
accident. He worried that something bad would happen to
them most of the time.

Although JF's symptoms were interfering with his ability
to get to school every morning, his parents were afraid to
have him take medication because he was so young. JF's worries about harm coming to his family made it difficult to
work with him alone, and so his parents were with him in
therapy for the first month. First, JF and his family were educated about obsessive-compulsive disorder, CBT, and E/RP.
They decided, with their therapist, to try CBT and E/RP for
six weeks to see if JF would start getting better without using
medication. The "E" in E/RP refers to the exposure principle
that says that anxiety will decrease after prolonged contact
with the feared stimulus in the absence of real threat. For
example, a person with a fear of heights goes up an elevator:
The first time, it is scary; the tenth time, it is boring. A person
with a fear of germs touches a dirty sink or floor and tolerates
the fear while trying not to wash his or her hands. After a
while, the fear starts to subside. The "RP" in E/RP refers to the
response prevention principle that states that adequate exposure is only possible in the absence of rituals or compulsions.
Not doing the ritual would involve refraining from handwashing after exposure—like when JF was hugged by his sister who had a cold. JF and his parents were instructed to
"make OCD the enemy," so they could fight the disorder
instead of each other. The family was given information on
how to work with JF's OCD symptoms to reduce the tension
at home. JF was asked to draw a picture of his OCD and write
a story about how it came to be. His drawing showed a huge,

Figure 8.2 A nine-year-old girl named Nicole drew this picture to show one of the symptoms of her anxiety—butterflies in her stomach—as she began treatment for her disorder.

robot-like, frightening monster. He then worked with his therapist to identify where the fear was in his body, so he could learn that fear is not dangerous even though it feels bad. Then he worked on learning to relax his body, especially the parts that felt most afraid.

JF was taught relaxation breathing and coping techniques, using humor to laugh at OCD as well as "fighting statements," such as "die OCD!" Younger children sometimes like to give OCD a nasty nickname such as "Yucky," "Germy," or "OCD Dummy." He and his therapist mapped his OCD, developed a symptom hierarchy of his fears, and rated them on a fear thermometer so they would know which fear would be easiest to fight first.

After six weeks, they had made some progress, but not enough. JF hated relaxation breathing and refused to practice it. He said it made him feel worse. He did like mobilizing imaginary army men to fight the battle against OCD, however, so his therapist devised a battle plan with fighter jet planes that JF brought from home to "blow up OCD." He still felt trapped by OCD most of the time, though, especially in school, where he was frequently teased and bullied about his need for cleanliness. At this point, his parents decided it was time to try an SSRI medication. JF was very upset at the idea of taking medication and said he would refuse to do so.

Several weeks later, after beginning medication treatment, JF said, "I never felt this good in my life!" He was smiling, less irritable, and better able to talk about his feelings. Still, he continued to struggle with many issues, especially in school. His teachers had difficulty understanding how his OCD symptoms interfered with his school performance. JF lived in a small suburb, and people in the community were aware of JF's irritable moods. Many felt he was just trying to get his way. A special meeting known as an individual education plan (IEP) was held at his school with the principal, teachers, school psychologist, special-education representative, JF's parents, and his therapist to develop a plan that would help JF be more successful in school. The school personnel were educated about OCD and accommodations were made for JF. His teachers were enlisted in the fight against OCD. They

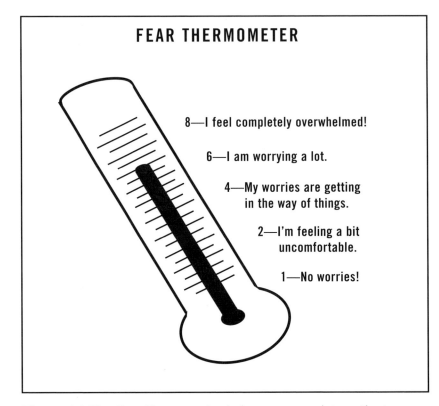

FEAR THERMOMETER

8—I feel completely overwhelmed!

6—I am worrying a lot.

4—My worries are getting
in the way of things.

2—I'm feeling a bit
uncomfortable.

1—No worries!

Figure 8.3 The Fear Thermometer helps young anxiety patients determine how afraid they are when exposed to the objects or situations they fear.

might be able to help by noticing if JF became "stuck" rereading the same sentence or page and encouraging him to move on.

JF's OCD symptoms began to subside. He and this therapist worked at decreasing his contamination fears. Together, they touched many contaminated surfaces—doorknobs, fire extinguishers, floors, toilet seats, and bathroom sinks. Once JF had contaminated his hands, they gradually increased his tolerance for the resulting fear or anxiety, and became able to wait for longer periods of time before washing his hands. His parents were instructed to stop carrying wet wipes and JF was encouraged to cope with his fear. He began to realize that no one was getting sick or dying just because he touched dirty surfaces.

Six months later, JF has improved greatly, but his war against OCD continues. The disorder suddenly resurfaces when JF is stressed, tired, or sick. He has therapy booster sessions each month to make sure that OCD never takes over his life again (although he knows his symptoms may get worse and better at various times). JF will remain on medicine for at least a year and perhaps longer. School continues to be a challenge for him. He sometimes behaves in an irritable, tense, curt manner when his anxiety is severe. JF longs to have more friends and has joined Boy Scouts and started swimming lessons.

CAUSES OF OCD

Although there are many ideas about what causes OCD, no single theory is universally accepted. Most experts agree that a combination of factors, both biological and psychological, contribute to the development of OCD. So, the cause of this disorder can best be understood using a "contributing factors" model. This simply means that a number of factors may lead to the onset of OCD. Some of the factors that have been proposed include:

- Infection with group A beta-hemolytic streptococci (a type of bacteria)
- Genetic predisposition
- Biochemical irregularities
- Stressful or traumatic life events

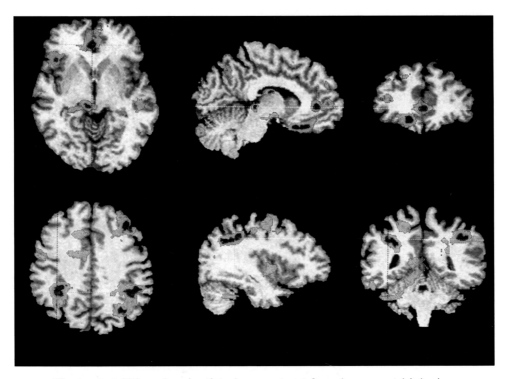

Figure 8.4 Although scientists have not yet found an exact biological cause for obsessive-compulsive disorder, certain tests, like this positron emission tomography (PET) scan, show that there are differences in the brains of people who suffer from OCD. This image shows activity in the brain of a person with OCD.

- History of childhood anxiety
- Family problems.

Research has focused on an infection-triggered cause in some cases of OCD and Tourette's syndrome/tic disorders that start in childhood. In some children, infections with certain streptococcal bacteria (like those that cause strep throat) may trigger an immune response against the bacteria but also produce an immune response that affects the brain area known as the basal ganglia. Initially, this causes damage to the basal ganglia that eventually goes away, but it may produce irreversible damage in some people. Some researchers believe treating the infection with antibiotics as quickly as possible may help prevent permanent damage to the brain. Children who develop OCD as a result of infection are identified by the acronym PANDAS (pediatric autoimmune neuropsychiatric disorders associated with streptococci).[40] A few cases have been reported that appear to have been triggered by viral infections.[41]

TREATMENT INTERVENTIONS FOR CHILDREN AND ADOLESCENTS WITH OCD

The first step in treating OCD is to educate the patient and his or her family about OCD. Over the last 20 years, two effective treatments for OCD have been developed: cognitive-behavioral psychotherapy (CBT) and the use of serotonin reuptake inhibitors (SSRIs). In the acute treatment phase, interventions are aimed at ending the current episode of OCD. This is followed by maintenance treatment that is aimed at preventing future episodes of OCD.

Components of Treatment

Education is crucial in helping patients and families learn how best to manage OCD and prevent its complications. CBT is the key element of treatment for most patients with OCD. Medication with a serotonin reuptake inhibitor is helpful for many patients.

Psychotherapy

CBT is the psychotherapeutic treatment of choice for children, adolescents, and adults with OCD. CBT helps the patient learn an effective strategy for resisting OCD that will be of lifelong benefit. Behavior therapy helps people learn to change their thoughts and feelings by first changing their behavior. Behavior therapy for OCD involves **exposure and response prevention (E/RP).**

Exposure is based on the fact that anxiety usually goes down after long enough contact with something that is feared. Thus, people with obsessions about germs are told to stay in contact with "germy" objects (for example, by handling money) until their anxiety is extinguished. The person's anxiety tends to decrease after repeated exposure until he or she no longer fears the contact.

For exposure to be of the most help, it needs to be combined with *response* or *ritual prevention* (RP). In RP, the person's rituals or avoidance behaviors are blocked. For example, people with excessive worries about germs must not only stay in contact with "germy things," but must also refrain from ritualized washing.

Exposure is generally more helpful in decreasing anxiety and obsessions, while response prevention is more helpful in decreasing compulsive behaviors. Despite years of struggling with OCD symptoms, many people have surprisingly little difficulty tolerating E/RP once they get started.

Cognitive therapy (CT) is a component of CBT. CT is often added to E/RP (Exposure/ritual prevention) to help reduce the catastrophic thinking and exaggerated sense of responsibility often seen in people with OCD. For example, a teenager with OCD may believe that his failure to remind his mother to wear a seat belt will cause her to die that day in a car accident. CT can help him challenge the faulty assumptions in this obsession. Armed with this proof, he will be better able to engage in E/RP—for example, by not calling his mother at work to make sure she arrived safely.

People react differently to psychotherapy, just as they do to medication. CBT is relatively free of side effects, but all patients will experience some amount of anxiety during treatment. CBT can be individual (just the patient and therapist), group (with other people), or family. A physician or nurse may provide both CBT and medication, or a psychologist or social worker may provide CBT, while a physician or nurse manages the medications.

Medication

Research clearly shows that the serotonin reuptake inhibitors (SSRIs) are the most effective medication treatments for OCD. Seven SSRIs are used for the treatment of OCD and are currently available by prescription in the United States:

- Clomipramine (Anafranil®)
- Fluoxetine (Prozac®)
- Fluvoxamine (Luvox®)
- Paroxetine (Paxil®)
- Sertraline (Zoloft®)
- Citalopram hydrobromide (Celexa®)
- Escitalopram oxalate (Lexapro®)

Of the medications listed, clomipramine is both an SSRI and a tricyclic antidepressant. It is very effective for OCD but has more side effects than other SSRIs. For this reason, the SSRIs are usually tried first, since people tend to tolerate them better.

Other Treatments

Forms of psychotherapy other than CBT can sometimes be helpful treatments for OCD. Support groups—meetings with other people who have the same problem—can also be useful. This can help patients feel they are not alone and they can discuss their struggles and strategies in fighting their

OCD with other people who are struggling with the same illness. Family involvement in the treatment process is often valuable, and sometimes essential.

Post-Traumatic Stress Disorder

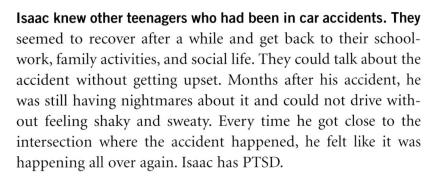

9

Isaac knew other teenagers who had been in car accidents. They seemed to recover after a while and get back to their schoolwork, family activities, and social life. They could talk about the accident without getting upset. Months after his accident, he was still having nightmares about it and could not drive without feeling shaky and sweaty. Every time he got close to the intersection where the accident happened, he felt like it was happening all over again. Isaac has PTSD.

STATISTICS

About 1% to 14% of the general population may develop **post-traumatic stress disorder** (**PTSD**) in their lifetime.[42] In one study, more than 40% of young people had experienced at least one severe trauma and more than 6% had PTSD by the age of 18.[43] Children and teenagers who are exposed to traumatic events such as rape, sexual or physical abuse, witnessing an accident or medical emergency, surviving cancer, or domestic violence are more likely to develop PTSD. Both Type I (one-time events) and Type II (repeated or long-standing exposure to events) traumas can result in PTSD in about one-quarter of young people exposed to them.[44]

There are gender and age differences in the development of PTSD. Girls may show more internalizing symptoms such as anxiety, sadness, and avoidance, while boys may show more

Figure 9.1 Post-Traumatic stress disorder (PTSD) occurs after a person is exposed to a stressful event, such as an accident, crime, or natural disaster. One of the worst traumatic events in recent history was the December 2004 tsunami that devastated parts of Asia. Mental health experts believe that up to 90% of the people who survived the tsunami may have suffered from PTSD.

externalizing symptoms such as aggression and hyperactivity.[45] Women have higher rates of PTSD than men. No child is too young to be at risk for PTSD. In fact, young children may be more sensitive to trauma than adolescents or adults.

PTSD is underreported and underdiagnosed in youth and can result in significant and chronic impairment. It may be difficult for young people to explain what they are feeling after a trauma, and they may not talk about the emotional impact with peers or parents. Adults may unknowingly downplay or deny the impact of the traumatic event.

CAUSES

Unlike most psychiatric disorders, PTSD has a specific cause that is usually a life-threatening trauma. However, many children who experience trauma do not develop PTSD. Scientists have been working to identify factors that may increase or decrease risk for developing PTSD after a trauma. Several factors put someone at risk for developing PTSD. Risk characteristics of the child include subjective sense of bodily or life threat, past history of traumas, coping style, anxiety, younger age, and female gender. Risk characteristics of the traumatic event include trauma with violence, direct physical harm, severity, duration, and the person's closeness to event. Characteristics of the family and social support system that decrease risk include a supportive and calm support system versus chaotic, distant, or anxious family communication that increases risk. Having predictable routines, a nurturing support system, and a sense of safety decrease a person's risk of developing PTSD.[46]

DIAGNOSIS

The current diagnosis of PTSD in children and adults in the United States is based on criteria in the DSM-IV. The diagnosis of PTSD requires exposure to a traumatic event or events that involve actual or possible death, injury, or threat to the physical well-being of oneself or others. A person with PTSD is very distressed by the trauma and shows it through emotions or behavior. Traumatic events that may lead to PTSD include witnessing someone die or get badly injured; serious car accidents; kidnapping; fire; natural disasters such as a hurricane; robbery or attack; sexual or physical abuse; and illnesses such as cancer or severe burns.

A person with PTSD reexperiences the traumatic event in at least one of the following ways. Upsetting thoughts or images of the trauma intrude into everyday activities. Frightening dreams or nightmares occur regularly and will not stop. The person acts or feels like the trauma is happening again. When reminded of the trauma, the person gets upset or overwhelmed, or has uncomfortable physical feelings such as a fast heartbeat, sweating, and shaking.

A person with PTSD avoids things that remind him or her of the trauma and experiences an overall numbing of feelings. This numbing occurs in several possible ways: It is hard to think about, talk about, or experience feelings related to the trauma. It is easier to avoid doing things, going places, or seeing people that serve as reminders of the trauma. It is hard to remember important things about the traumatic event. Things that used to be fun (such as playing games or hobbies) are no longer interesting and are avoided after the trauma. There is a loss of interest in seeing friends, and it is difficult to get close to family or friends again. It is hard to show feelings to other people. It seems that the future will not work out—the person has trouble thinking of future events, such as finishing school, getting a job, or getting married.

A person with PTSD experiences increased arousal or feels "keyed up" after the trauma. It may be hard for the person to fall asleep or stay asleep. He or she gets angry or often feels irritable, even over small things. The person has trouble concentrating, which may affect school performance or participation in extracurricular activities. A person with PTSD is often on the "lookout" to be ready if something happens (this is called hypervigilance). When something happens by surprise, like hearing an unexpected loud noise, the person is jumpy and gets startled easily.

For a diagnosis of PTSD, the disturbance must be present for more than one month and must cause significant problems or interfere with important aspects of life such as friendships, school, work, or relationships with family. The disorder stops the patient from doing things he or she would like to do. PTSD is classified as acute when symptoms have been present for less than three months, or chronic when symptoms have been present for more than three months. In some cases, PTSD can have a delayed onset—the symptoms do not start until at least six months after the traumatic event takes place. **Acute stress disorder** is diagnosed if most of the criteria for PTSD are met, but the disturbance lasts for a minimum of two days and a maximum of one month and occurs within one month of the traumatic event.

CASE STUDY

Isaac was a 17-year-old high school student who was in a very serious car accident nine months ago. Isaac was driving his friend Thomas home after soccer practice at school. They were caught in a downpour and a car skidded out of control right in front of them at an intersection. Isaac did his best to stop as quickly as he could, but he was unable to avoid a head-on collision. Isaac and Thomas were knocked unconscious for a brief period and were taken by ambulance to the hospital after another motorist called 911. Isaac remembers the ambulance ride and being overwhelmed and horrified by the severe pain from his injuries and by seeing all the blood that covered his friend. Thomas had not been wearing his seat belt and crashed through the windshield, which led him to suffer serious injuries.

Isaac remained in the hospital for several days, then went through several months of physical therapy. He was able to attend school during physical therapy but needed some help from other students until he got back his strength. He had some scars but was fortunate to have such a good physical recovery. Thomas was not so lucky. He suffered a serious head injury that affected his ability to speak and caused problems with his learning and memory. Thomas had been an excellent student, but now he needed a special-educational program at school. He had always had a positive attitude and maintained this characteristic even after the accident. He made the most of the rehabilitative services he was provided and the support he received from his family and friends. He remained determined to pursue his goals in high school and in the future.

Isaac seemed to adjust well initially after the accident and focused on his physical recovery. Within two months, however, he began to have repeated nightmares about the accident. In his dreams, he often survived and his friend died. He recalled the horror of the ambulance ride and his friend being covered in blood. He often woke up in a panic from the nightmares and was afraid to go back to sleep. As months went by he looked tired all the time, but he was on edge, as if he were waiting for something bad to happen. Noises that would not have bothered him in the past, such as police sirens, car alarms, and loud whistles by the referee at his soccer game, now made him jump and shiver with fear. Whenever he approached the intersection where the accident occurred, he felt as if another crash might happen. He began to feel afraid to drive and had to be driven places by his friends or parents. Things that were red in color reminded him of the blood at the accident scene. Whenever he saw something red, his heart would beat faster and he would feel shaky.

Isaac's family and friends grew concerned when he began to keep more to himself and avoid activities that reminded him of the accident, such as soccer and driving. He began to express guilt about not making Thomas wear his seat belt. He felt he could have prevented his friend's injuries if he had been more concerned about his safety and had been able to stop the car faster. He did not respond when his parents or friends urged him to be more reasonable, telling him that he had done his best. Thomas tried to reassure Isaac, too, but Isaac could not let go of the self-blame. Over time, Isaac detached from people in his life and no longer showed the range of feelings he once did. He stopped enjoying things that were usually fun. He found it hard to look forward to his future and was not sure if he would graduate from high school. He had trouble concentrating in school and while doing his homework. His grades dropped. He denied having suicidal thoughts but expressed little hope about his future.

Six months after the accident, Isaac's family expressed their concerns to their family physician, Dr. Patel. Dr. Patel performed a physical exam and did some bloodwork to rule out any specific medical concerns. He did note that Isaac had lost some weight and looked very tired and worn out. Dr. Patel could not find any physical abnormalities but felt Isaac might be getting depressed and that this had led to a decreased appetite and sleep problems. Dr. Patel referred Isaac to a child and adolescent psychiatrist for a full evaluation based on the severity of his problems. Dr. Patel was worried about Isaac's hopelessness regarding the future. The doctor prescribed an SSRI medication due to his concerns about depression and helped get Isaac an appointment at the University Child Psychiatry Clinic. Dr. Patel told the family about possible side effects and the need to monitor for suicidal ideas. He agreed to see them regularly to check on the medication until Isaac saw the new doctor.

Isaac was not eager to talk with another doctor about his problems but agreed to do so at his parents' request. He was most concerned that he was losing weight and not sleeping well, especially with the bad nightmares. Dr. Murphy met with Isaac and his parents together to gather information about his illness, early history, family, social functioning, and school functioning. She reviewed information she got from

Dr. Patel about Isaac's physical exam, weight changes, and bloodwork. Dr. Murphy had Isaac fill out questionnaires about his anxiety, depression, social support, coping skills, and family life. She also collected questionnaires about Isaac from his parents, and with the family's permission, from Isaac's school. Dr. Murphy also met with Isaac alone to understand the severity of his symptoms better and how they were affecting his life at home, with friends, and at school. Isaac shared some suicidal thoughts that had started in the past month before he started the SSRI medication. He had been afraid to tell anyone about this before, but he thought it was important to do so now.

Dr. Murphy made a diagnosis of PTSD and **major depression**. She explained the combination of medication and psychotherapy that she felt would be best, based on Isaac's symptoms. She was glad that Dr. Patel had already started the SSRI medication. Dr. Murphy also considered adding guanfacine or clonidine to help Isaac with his recurrent nightmares, restlessness, and feelings of being "on edge" all the time. She would monitor Isaac's heart, blood pressure, and pulse while he took the new medicine. Dr. Murphy encouraged Isaac to discuss his suicidal thoughts with his parents, and they developed a plan in case his thoughts got worse and he thought he might try to hurt himself. Isaac felt relieved to share his feelings. He was glad to know that such thoughts were common with depression, especially when it happened after a severe trauma. Isaac and his family agreed to continue treatment at the clinic until Isaac's anxiety and depression were more stable and he could switch to treatment closer to home.

At the clinic, Isaac worked with a therapist every week to receive cognitive-behavioral therapy (CBT) and saw Dr. Murphy for his medications. As his mood and suicidal thoughts improved a little, Isaac was able to work on learning new ways of coping such as relaxation, positive self-talk, and problem-solving skills. Strategies that helped him included deep breathing, relaxing different muscles, and thinking of a relaxing place. He enjoyed taking deep breaths and thinking about lying on the beach his family visited every summer, looking up at the blue sky on a warm day. He could smell the fresh air and hear the birds chirping and trees rustling. He came up with some positive things he could say to himself when he was feeling down. He learned how to tell when he was starting to feel anxious rather than waiting until he felt overwhelmed. He became aware of how physical sensations in his body could help him to identify his anxiety and other feelings. He started to rate his anxiety each day and practiced his relaxation strategies until he was confident about using them.

Isaac then participated in exposure, imagining the steps of the car accident in his mind and describing them to the therapist. He was asked to rate his anxiety from 0 (no distress) to 10 (as upset as he had ever been) at each step in telling his story. Each time his anxiety got high, he stopped and used his relaxation strategies to bring it down. Once he was calm, he went on with the story. It took Isaac a number of sessions to get through the whole story. It felt overwhelming at times and it took all of his effort to calm himself, even with the therapist's help. For a while, as he began to tell his story in detail, he experienced a worsening in his nightmares and renewed fears that a bad accident could happen again soon, and he appeared more withdrawn. His therapist explained that this was part of the process of working through his frightening memories of the trauma and that, ultimately, he would be able to tell the story or think of the accident without feeling overwhelmed and upset. Isaac's family learned strategies to help him calm down and also learned the relaxation strategies and coping skills needed to assist him. It was important that they not get upset or appear frightened themselves when he needed their help to calm himself. This was not always easy, since his parents remembered how happy and full of life he had been before the accident. At times, they worried that they would never get their son back. His parents provided Isaac with lots of positive feedback for his courage in working on his fears and tolerating his distress during the treatment process.

Once his anxiety about the memories of the accident was reduced, Isaac was able to discuss the guilt he felt over the accident and his friend's injuries. He was also able to look at how he felt the accident had affected his life and his thoughts about the future. The therapist was able to help him bring these thoughts back to normal and think about what he could do to reach his goals and get back to his usual activities. He worked through things that triggered the trauma, such as rainy weather, seeing the color red, or driving by the intersection where the accident had happened. He practiced using his new coping strategies to tolerate these situations and slowly got comfortable with them again so that he was no longer afraid of them and no longer felt the need to avoid them. Eventually, Isaac was able to watch movies that had car crash scenes. He worked with his parents to practice driving again and slowly regained his confidence. He was able to earn positive rewards that he chose with his parents, such as music CDs, for practicing his coping skills and completing steps in his exposure plan. He used tape recordings of his sessions to practice at home as well.

Isaac was able to resume most of his normal activities after several months in treatment. He continued to see his therapist and doctor once a month for a year to maintain his gains. He received booster sessions when the anniversary of the accident approached or when triggers such as news events of serious accidents caused his fears to briefly get worse. Over time he learned how to cope with and prepare for these problems. When his anxiety and depression were stable for a year, his doctor tried reducing his medications slowly, but Isaac experienced some increase in his worries and sad feelings. They found it helped him to remain on a lower dose of the medication for another six months, and then he was able to tolerate a slow discontinuation of the medication. Isaac finished high school with his classmates and went on to pursue his goals for the future. Interestingly, he eventually worked in management at a car manufacturing plant, having conquered his fears related to the trauma.

ADDITIONAL CHARACTERISTICS

PTSD can occur with different symptoms at different ages and stages of development in children and adolescents.[47] Infants may be irritable, show sleep problems, or have diarrhea and frequent illnesses. Preschoolers may show increased difficulty separating from parents, irritability, bedwetting, traumatic themes in their play, and sleep problems. Elementary schoolchildren may show more typical PTSD symptoms. Physical symptoms may decrease as children get older. Their behavior may change often from withdrawn to friendly to aggressive or irritable. Teenagers may be very compliant and withdrawn, or aggressive, and may display substance abuse and sexual acting-out behavior. Teenagers may show new separation anxiety after a traumatic event and have difficulty sleeping in their own rooms. Survivor guilt may be more severe in teenagers with PTSD who believe that they should have done more to help others survive, even if this was not realistic under the circumstances. PTSD can

Figure 9.2 A severe anxiety disorder can impact everything in the patient's life and can lead to depression and other mental health problems. This picture, drawn by a young anxiety patient named Kenyetta, depicts her struggle with anxiety and depression.

block or slow down the process of grieving a traumatic loss in significant ways.[48] Just thinking about the loss can trigger PTSD symptoms that are overwhelming and make it hard to work through grief, anger, sadness, or eventual acceptance of the loss and move on with one's life.

Traumatic experiences may lead to significant activity changes in the brains of children and adolescents. This can result in: 1) difficulties concentrating on schoolwork; 2) effects on memory that affect new learning and previously learned material; 3) elevated stress hormones that may be toxic to the developing brain and have an impact on brain growth; and 4) increased psychiatric and physical illness.

CO-OCCURRING DISORDERS

PTSD commonly occurs at the same time as other psychiatric disorders. Major depression is the most common co-occurring disorder, especially when PTSD has not been identified or treated and continues into teenage years. Other common co-occurring conditions include anxiety disorders such as social anxiety, specific phobia, generalized anxiety disorder, and panic disorder. Substance use disorders such as alcohol dependence and drug dependence also co-occur in teenagers. Teens who have survived physical abuse may experience high levels of depression and suicidal thoughts, and be at risk for drug overdose. Those who have experienced repeated traumas may have a higher risk for self-injury and dissociative disorders. Young people with dissociative disorders feel detached from themselves, feel like they are not in "real life," or may not remember important events or information. "Tuning out" the emotional or physical experience may have helped the child or teenager survive and get through the trauma. Once the trauma is over, this dissociation may continue and require treatment.

Many children and teenagers with PTSD become irritable and angry with parents, teachers, and peers, or become unusually aggressive without a clear trigger. Reminders of the trauma may be evident to the teenager with PTSD but not to others. Young people with PTSD need proper diagnosis because the symptoms of PTSD, such as restlessness and poor concentration, may overlap with other disorders such as attention-deficit/hyperactivity disorder (ADHD) and other anxiety disorders. Behavior disorders such as ADHD may also co-occur with PTSD.

INTERVENTIONS

Treatment of PTSD in children and adolescents often involves multiple approaches that start with psychotherapy and parental guidance, and can include medications, group therapy, and family therapy when appropriate. Early intervention is very important. The treatment approach needs to consider the nature of the trauma (whether it is acute or chronic) and the child's support system.[49]

It is crucial to have a good diagnostic evaluation by a health professional who can consider any possible medical causes for the PTSD symptoms and who is familiar with evaluating children and adolescents. A physical exam is important, especially in cases of abuse, neglect, or physical injury, to determine the extent of the physical trauma, collect evidence for a forensic evaluation to be used in a court of law, and rule out medical conditions that may be present. Some children with PTSD may have higher than normal pulse or blood pressure, which is part of their body's response to the trauma.

The first step in the treatment of PTSD is to establish a stable, safe, predictable environment. This may not be easy to do in a number of Type II traumas where there is ongoing abuse or violence between family members in the home. Numerous adults—from supportive family members to police, community agencies, child protective services, and school personnel—may need to get involved to reach this goal. This step is critical in reducing the impact of ongoing trauma.

Once safety is established, the child or teenager can make better use of therapy and other interventions and feel comfortable enough to express past traumas and fears. A teenager with PTSD may initially appear withdrawn, quiet, emotionally numb, or overly compliant with adults, and may complain of various aches and pains. As progress is made in treatment, the patient may begin to discuss the trauma and express anger, sadness, opposition, irritability, and fear, and display appropriate emotional needs or demands for the first time. This may, on the surface, seem to be a decline or worsening in behavior and put additional stress on family members. However, it may be a first step toward psychological health and recovery in gaining trust and self-awareness, and processing the traumatic experience rather than less optimal avoidance or withdrawal.[50] It is critical to support young people and their families through this process.

There are several aspects of psychotherapy that are useful in the treatment of youth with PTSD.[51] Relaxation and desensitization strategies can help the child with overwhelming anxiety related to the trauma. The trauma is discussed in detail at a pace that is comfortable. The therapy challenges thoughts related to the traumatic event, such as "It was my fault" and "Nothing is safe anymore." Parents or other supportive adults are involved in treatment to monitor the child or teenager, learn behavioral strategies for difficult situations related to the PTSD behavior, and provide information about PTSD. Parents are also encouraged to get the help they need to manage their own recovery from the trauma so that they can be calm and supportive for their child.

The goals of trauma-focused cognitive behavioral therapy (CBT) are to reduce symptoms of PTSD, teach positive coping skills, and increase a sense of control and well-being. CBT uses gradual exposures to traumatic memories, thoughts, or reminders in the mind (imaginal) and in real life (live exposure) to allow emotional processing of the traumatic memories in such a way that they are no longer overwhelming.[52]

Other non-exposure-based talk therapies, family therapy, and non-CBT-based group therapy have shown some benefits in clinical studies but need to be researched further in children and teenagers. Often, several treatment approaches are combined to address the individual needs of the child or family. Very little data exists to guide the medication treatment of PTSD in children and teenagers, and no definitive recommendations can be made. However, medications may be used along with psychotherapy to help the PTSD recovery process by reducing the severity of symptoms and impairment in the child's life. Medications may allow the child to tolerate participation in psychotherapy without overwhelming fear, anxiety, or hyperarousal. Medications can also target co-occurring anxiety and depressive disorders, improve sleep, decrease intrusive thoughts, and limit avoidance.[53] Studies in adults with PTSD favor antidepressants with serotonin reuptake inhibitors (SSRIs). Clinical studies in children are limited but have also shown positive results for SSRIs. Other types of medications being studied are clonidine and guanfacine, which may reduce hyperarousal symptoms such as impulsivity, startle responses, and nightmares. Antipsychotic medications or neuroleptics which work on dopamine receptors in the brain may be considered in severe situations when a child or adolescent suffers from an acute worsening of PTSD and experiences dissociation or psychotic symptoms, or has difficulty distinguishing past traumas from present reality. At such times, an adolescent may act out with severe aggression, struggle with severe sleep problems, or actively complain of distressing intrusive thoughts, hearing voices, or seeing things others do not (hallucinations), and show poor judgment that places him or her at risk for harm to him- or herself or others.

Outlook for the Future

We have learned a great deal about the evaluation and treatment of anxiety disorders in children and teenagers over the past decade. There is still a great deal to learn and understand. Current research is examining risk and protective factors that may help us identify anxiety in young children and provide interventions early in life. It is hoped that this can prevent the development of severe anxiety disorders and reduce the serious impact of these disorders on both children and adults. In addition, scientists are comparing treatment with SSRI medications and CBT to better understand when each of these interventions should be used. Over the next decade, it will be important to make effective screening and treatment tools for anxiety disorders more readily available. One way to do this is by providing more training for health professionals to allow them to identify anxiety disorders in young people and to use effective treatments.

Despite being very common, anxiety disorders are currently very much underidentified in children and adolescents relative to other psychiatric disorders. It is our hope that this book will provide young people with an introduction to the symptoms and treatment of anxiety disorders so they will be better informed and realize that effective treatments are available.

Bill's Story

Excerpts from "Untitled Existence," written by a patient with anxiety and depression

I decided that it was getting out of hand. I made that big leap, took a deep breath, and asked my parents to get me help. I began seeing a psychologist nearby to my house. The sessions were interesting at first, but I wasn't ready to tell anyone what I really thought. The care stagnated. Though I was trying to work it out on my own, I didn't have the correct tools to do it. I was trying to swim while simultaneously holding a large rock and it wasn't working out.

I decided I would go back to school. I was telling myself that I was getting better, after all, and normal kids go to school every day. But I wasn't really getting better. On the eve of my first day back I had a panic attack. . . . I couldn't stop pacing or speaking, my breathing was coming heavy now and I didn't know why. To be very clear I was not trying to do any of this. I wanted with my entire conscious mind to stop it. I wanted to know that everything was going to be alright. But everything wasn't alright; my coping mechanisms were gone and I didn't know what to do with my emotions. I didn't even know how to recognize them.

. . . I'd been fighting for too many years. I'd been fighting too hard. I'd been fighting through my life without understanding the problem. Sitting in that chair, my life changed because for the first time I let someone with the proper understanding start making the decisions. I stopped fighting the help and let the help help me start fighting the battle.

By no definition was I cured. In my future were many doctors' visits, a slew of new drugs, and the question "How does that make you feel." For months I would take two steps forward and one step back. And each time I would get upset and then remind myself that I was one step closer to my goal.

As I write, I am sitting in a new school surrounded by new friends. We are enjoying an hour between classes. I am now better able to understand my family—not to change them, I'm no longer trying to do that, just to understand how my family works. I have gone from quitting all my sports and clubs to starting them. Just this year I will hold an officer position in six of the clubs I am a member of.

I made an abrupt 180 on life. Not because I "pulled myself up by the boot straps" or because I "found god" or even because "I got some distance." I have helped myself through the aid afforded to me by the psychiatrists, psychologists, therapists, friends, relatives, and programs that have offered to help me. I am proud to say that my recovery was a group effort. It's a slippery slope out there; luckily, I have lots of people willing to push me back up.

NOTES

1. Dadds, M. R., D. E. Holland, K. P. Laurens, M. Mullins, P. M. Barrett, and S. H. Spence. "Early Intervention and Prevention of Anxiety Disorders in Children: Results at Two-year Follow-up." *Journal of Consulting and Clinical Psychology* 67 (1999): 145–150.

2. Pine, D. S., P. Cohen, D. Gurley, J. Brook, and Y. Ma "The Risk for Early-Adulthood Anxiety and Depressive Disorders in Adolescents with Anxiety and Depressive Disorders." *Archives of General Psychiatry* 55 (1998): 56–64.

3. Bogels, S. M., and D. Zigterman. "Dysfunctional Cognitions in Children With Social Phobia, Separation Anxiety Disorder, and Generalized Anxiety Disorder." *Journal of Abnormal Child Psychology* 28 (2000): 205–211.

4. Ialongo, N., G. Edelsohn, L. Werthamer-Larsson, L. Crockett, and S. Kellam, "The Significance of Self-reported Anxious Symptoms in First Grade Children: Prediction to Anxious Symptoms and Adaptive Functioning in Fifth Grade." *Journal of Child Psychology and Psychiatry* 36 (1995): 427–437.

5. Woodward, L. J., and D. M. Fergusson. "Life Course Outcomes of Young People with Anxiety Disorders in Adolescence." *Journal of the American Academy of Child and Adolescent Psychiatry* 40 (2001): 1086–1093.

6. Spence, S. H. "Prevention Strategies". *The Developmental Psychopathology of Anxiety*, ed. M. W. Vasey and M. R. Dadds. Oxford: Oxford University Press, 2001.

7. Kagan, J., and N. Snidman. "Early Childhood Predictors of Adult Anxiety Disorders." *Biological Psychiatry* 46 (1999): 1536–1541.

8. Dadds, M. R., and J. H. Roth. "Family Processes in the Development of Anxiety Problems." *The Developmental Psychopathology of Anxiety*, ed. M. W. Vasey and M.R. Dadds. Oxford: Oxford University Press, 2001.

9. Spence, S. H. "Prevention Strategies". *The Developmental Psychopathology of Anxiety*, ed. M. W. Vasey and M. R. Dadds. Oxford: Oxford University Press, 2001.

10. Ayers, T. S., I. N. Sandler, S. G. West, and M. W. Roosa. "A Dispositional and Situational Assessment of Children's Coping: Testing Alternative Models of Coping." *Journal of Personality* 64(4) (1996): 923–958.

11. Albano, A.M., and P. C. Kendall. "Cognitive Behavioural Therapy for Children and Adolescents With Anxiety Disorders: Clinical Research Advances." *International Review of Psychiatry* 14 (2002): 129–134.

12. Ollendick, T. H., and J. March J. "Integrated Psychosocial and Pharmacological Treatment." *Phobic and Anxiety Disorders in Children and Adolescents*, ed. T. H. Ollendick and J. S. March. New York: Oxford University Press, 2004.

13. Costello, E. J., H. L. Egger, and A. Angold. "Developmental Epidemiology of Anxiety Disorders." *Phobic and Anxiety Disorders in Children and Adolescents*, ed. T. H. Ollendick and J. S. March. New York: Oxford University Press, 2004.

14. Kendall P. C., S. Pimentel, M. A. Rynn, A. Angelosante, and A. Webb. "Generalized Anxiety Disorder." *Phobic and Anxiety Disorders in Children and Adolescents*, ed. T. H. Ollendick and J. S. March. New York: Oxford University Press, 2004.

15. Masi, G., M. Mucci, L. Favilla, R. Romano, and P. Poli. "Symptomatology and Comorbidity of Generalized Anxiety Disorder in Children and Adolescents." *Comprehensive Psychiatry* 40 (1999): 210–215.

16. Levin, M., S. Ashmore-Callahan, P. Kendall, and M. Ichii (1996). "Treatment of Separation Anxiety Disorder." *Cognitive Therapy with Children and Adolescents*, ed. M. Reinecke, F. Dattilio, and A. Freeman. New York: Guilford Press, 1996.

17. Ibid.

18. Cronk, N. J., W. S. Slutske, P. A. F. Madden, K. K. Bucholz, and A. C. Heath. "Risk for Separation Anxiety Disorder Among Girls: Parental Absence, Socioeconomic Disadvantage, and Genetic Vulnerability." *Journal of Abnormal Psychology* 113 (2004): 237–247.

19. American Psychiatric Association. *Diagnostic and Statistical Manual of Mental Disorders*, Edition 4 (DSM-IV). Washington, DC: American Psychiatric Association Press, 1994.

20. Albano, A. M., B. F. Chorpita, and D. H. Barlow. "Childhood Anxiety Disorders." Child Psychopathology, ed. E. J. Mash and R. A. Barkley. New York: Guilford Press, 2003: 279–329.

21. Levin, M., S. Ashmore-Callahan, P. Kendall, and M. Ichii M (1996). "Treatment of Separation Anxiety Disorder." *Cognitive Therapy with Children and Adolescents*, ed. M. Reinecke, F. Dattilio, and A. Freeman. New York: Guilford Press, 1996.

22. Albano, A. M., B. F. Chorpita, and D. H. Barlow. "Childhood Anxiety Disorders." *Child Psychopathology*, ed. E. J. Mash and R. A. Barkley. New York: Guilford Press, 2003: 279–329.

23. Beidel, D. C., S. M. Turner, and T. L. Morris. "Psychopathology of Childhood Social Phobia." *Journal of the American Academy of Child and Adolescent Psychiatry* 38 (1999): 643–650.

24. Albano, A. M., B. F. Chorpita, and D. H. Barlow. "Childhood Anxiety Disorders." *Child Psychopathology*, ed. E. J. Mash and R. A. Barkley. New York: Guilford Press, 2003: 279–329.

25. Ibid.

26. Ibid.

27. Ibid.

28. Ginsburg, G. S., and J. T. Walkup. "Specific Phobia." *Phobic and Anxiety Disorders in Children and Adolescents*, ed. T. H. Ollendick and J. S. March. New York: Oxford University Press, 2004.

29. King, N. J., P. Muris, and T. H. Ollendick. "Specific Phobia." *Anxiety Disorders in Children and Adolescents*, 2nd edition. Ed. T. L. Morris and J. S. March. New York: Guilford Press, 2004.

30. Ginsburg, G. S., and J. T. Walkup. "Specific Phobia." *Phobic and Anxiety*

Disorders in Children and Adolescents, ed. T. H. Ollendick and J. S. March. New York: Oxford University Press, 2004.

31. Albano, A. M., B. F. Chorpita, and D. H. Barlow. "Childhood Anxiety Disorders." *Child Psychopathology*, ed. E. J. Mash and R. A. Barkley. New York: Guilford Press, 2003: 279–329.

32. Ollendick, T. H. "Panic disorder in Children and Adolescents: New Developments, New Directions." *Journal of Clinical Child Psychology* 27 (1998): 234–245.

33. Albano, A. M., B. F. Chorpita, and D. H. Barlow. "Childhood Anxiety Disorders." *Child Psychopathology*, ed. E. J. Mash and R. A. Barkley. New York: Guilford Press, 2003: 279–329.

34. Biederman, J., S. V. Farane, D. R. Hirshfeld-Becker, D. Friedman, J. A. Robin, and J. F. Rosenbaum. "Patterns of Psychopathology and Dysfunction in High-Risk Children of Parents with Panic Disorder and Major Depression." *American Journal of Psychiatry* 158 (2001): 49–57.

35. Albano, A. M., B. F. Chorpita, and D. H. Barlow. "Childhood Anxiety Disorders." *Child Psychopathology*, ed. E. J. Mash and R. A. Barkley. New York: Guilford Press, 2003: 279–329.

36. Ibid.; Essau, C. A., J. Conradt, and F. Petermann. "Frequency of Panic Attacks and Panic Disorder in Adolescents." *Depression and Anxiety* 9 (1999): 19–26.

37. Kearney, C. A., A. M. Albano, A. R. Eisen, W. D. Allan, and D. H. Barlow. "The Phenomenology of Panic Disorder in Youngsters: An Empirical Study of a Clinical Sample." *Journal of Anxiety Disorders* 11 (1997): 49–63.

38. Birmaher, B., and T. H. Ollendick. "Childhood-Onset Panic Disorder." *Phobic and Anxiety Disorders in Children and Adolescents*, ed. T. H. Ollendick and J. S. March. New York: Oxford University Press, 2004.

39. March, J. S., H. L. Leonard, and S. E. Swedo. "Anxiety Disorders in Children and Adolescents." *Obsessive-Compulsive Disorder*. New York: Guilford Press, 1995.

40. Swedo, S. E., H. L. Leonard, B. Mittleman, et al. (1997). "Identification of Children with Pediatric Autoimmune Neuropsychiatric Disorders Associated with Streptococcal Infections by a Marker Associated with Rheumatic Fever." *American Journal of Psychiatry* 154 (1997): 110–112.

41. Allen, A. J., H. L. Leonard, and S. E. Swedo. "Case Study: A New Infection-Triggered, Autoimmune Subtype of Pediatric OCD and Tourette's Syndrome." *Journal of the American Academy of Child & Adolescent Psychiatry* 34(3) (1995): 307–311.

42. American Psychiatric Association. *Diagnostic and Statistical Manual of Mental Disorders*, Edition 4 (DSM IV). Washington, DC: American Psychiatric Association Press, 1994.

43. Giaconia, R. M., H. Z. Reinherz, A. B. Silverman, B. Pakiz, A. K. Frost, and E. Cohen. "Traumas and Posttraumatic

Stress Disorder in a Community Population of Older Adolescents." *Journal of the American Academy of Child and Adolescent Psychiatry* 34 (1995): 1369–1380.

44. McCloskey, L. A., and M. Walker. "Posttraumatic Stress in Children Exposed to Family Violence and Single-Event Trauma." *Journal of the American Academy of Child and Adolescent Psychiatry* 26(5) (2000): 764–769.

45. Ackerman, P. T., J. E. Newton, W. B. McPherson, J. G. Jones, and R. A. Dykman. "Prevalence of Posttraumatic Stress Disorder and Other Psychiatric Diagnoses in Three Groups of Abused Children (Sexual, Physical, and Both)." *Child Abuse and Neglect* 22 (1998): 759–774.

46. Perry, B. D., and I. Azad. "Posttraumatic Stress Disorders in Children and Adolescents." *Current Opinion in Pediatrics* 11(4) (1999): 310–320.

47. Perrin, S., P. Smith, and W. Yule. "Practitioner Review: The Assessment and Treatment of Post-Traumatic Stress Disorder in Children and Adolescents." *Journal Child Psychology & Psychiatry* 41(3) (2000): 277–289.

48. Pynoos, R. S. (1992). "Grief and Trauma in Children and Adolescents." *Bereavement Care*, 2 (1992) 2–10.

49. Pynoos, R., and K. Nader. "Prevention of Psychiatric Morbidity in Children and Disaster." *Disaster Information: A Resource Kit*, ed. R. Pynoos and K. Nader. American Academy of Child and Adolescent Psychiatry Press, 1990.

50. Davies, W. H., and D. J. Flannery. "Post-Traumatic Stress Disorders in Children and Adolescents Exposed to Violence: Violence Among Children and Adolescents." *Pediatric Clinics of North America* 45(2) (1998): 341–353.

51. Cohen, J. A. "American Academy of Child and Adolescent Psychiatry Official Action: Practice Parameters for the Assessment and Treatment of Children and Adolescents With Posttraumatic Stress Disorder." *Journal of the American Academy of Child and Adolescent Psychiatry* 37 (10 supplement) (1998): 4S–26S.

52. Perrin, S., P. Smith, and W. Yule. "Practitioner Review: The Assessment and Treatment of Post-Traumatic Stress Disorder in Children and Adolescents." *Journal Child Psychology & Psychiatry* 41(3) (2000): 277–289.

53. McKnight, C. D., S. N. Compton, and J. S. March. "Posttraumatic Stress Disorder." *Anxiety Disorders in Children and Adolescents*, 2nd edition. Ed. T. L. Morris and J. S. March. New York: Guilford Press, 2004.

GLOSSARY

Acute stress disorder—An anxiety disorder that follows an extremely traumatic event and is similar to post-traumatic stress disorder but lasts only up to one month and has fewer symptoms.

Agoraphobia—An anxiety disorder characterized by avoidance of particular places or social settings, such as crowds, for fear of being unable to escape or obtain help if necessary. Agoraphobia is often, but not always, associated with fear of experiencing panic attacks.

Attention-deficit/hyperactivity disorder (ADHD)—A psychiatric disorder that starts in childhood and includes difficulties with concentration or hyperactivity and impulsivity.

Avoidant coping—Avoiding a feared object or situation rather than facing it directly.

Behavioral inhibition—A temperamental style characterized by shyness, caution, emotional restraint, and tendency to avoid new situations.

Benzodiazepines—A class of drugs that have tranquilizing or sleep-inducing properties.

Bipolar disorder—A mood disorder in children and adults that includes periods of abnormally elevated or irritable mood that may alternate with depression.

Co-occurring disorder—A disorder that happens along with the illness that is the focus of attention.

Cognitive-behavioral therapy (CBT)—When used to treat anxiety disorders, in CBT, the child or teenager learns relaxation and coping skills and is given opportunities to practice these skills with exposures to develop a sense of control and mastery in everyday situations that may normally provoke anxiety.

Compulsions—Repetitive behaviors or mental acts used to relieve the distress and anxiety caused by obsessions. Also called rituals.

Electrocardiogram (EKG)—A tracing of the electrical activity of the heart.

Exposure—A part of cognitive-behavioral therapy where a person with anxiety is asked to think about or come in contact with anxiety-producing objects or situations.

Exposure and response prevention (E/RP)—A type of therapy in which contact with a feared object or situation is combined with response prevention in which the person's rituals or avoidance behaviors are blocked during the exposure.

Family therapy—A type of treatment that looks at patterns of behavior in the family rather than focusing on an individual person.

Fear hierarchy—A list of situations or objects that rates them from least anxiety-producing to most anxiety-producing.

Generalized anxiety disorder—An anxiety disorder that involves daily, uncontrollable, and excessive worry that is associated with a range of things and situations.

Imaginal exposure—Exposure in which the anxiety-producing situation or object is imagined in the patient's mind or by looking at pictures or models of the object.

Interoceptive exposure—Exposure to physical symptoms associated with panic attacks by using exercises that induce these sensations.

In-vivo exposure (live exposure)—Exposure to the real-life situation or object; usually carried out once imaginal exposures feel comfortable and the patient is using coping skills successfully.

Major depression—A mood disorder in which there is depressed or irritable mood or loss of interest or pleasure nearly every day for at least two weeks. This is accompanied by symptoms such as changes in appetite, sleep, energy level, or activity level; feelings of worthlessness; or thoughts of death.

Modeling—An exposure therapy technique in which a patient learns to be less fearful by observing other people handling the feared objects and situations with good coping behavior through films or videotapes (symbolic models) or in real life (live models) with therapist, parent, or other children.

Neurotransmitter—A substance in the brain that is used for communication between brain cells (neurons).

Obsessions—Unpleasant, uncontrollable thoughts, impulses, or images that create fear or distress and get stuck in a person's mind and are replayed over and over.

Obsessive-compulsive disorder—A disorder with either excessive or unreasonable obsessions, compulsions, or both that cause marked distress, are time consuming, or interfere with normal functioning.

Panic attacks—Discrete episodes of intense fear or discomfort accompanied by several physical and/or cognitive symptoms.

Panic disorder—An anxiety disorder with repeated panic attacks that appear from "out of the blue" with persistent concern about having additional attacks or worry about the implication of the attack or its consequences.

Participant modeling—An exposure therapy technique in which the therapist helps the patient directly approach a feared object or situation.

Positive reinforcement—Rewarding someone for positive behavior.

Post-Traumatic stress disorder—An anxiety disorder that occurs after exposure to an extremely traumatic event and includes symptoms of reexperiencing the trauma, avoidance or numbing, and increased arousal.

Prevalence—The number of cases of an illness that exist at a certain time in a certain area.

Protective factors—Factors that strengthen psychological health and counteract the impact of risk factors.

Psychotherapy—A type of treatment that involves verbal or nonverbal communication (e.g., talk therapy).

Risk factors—Factors that increase the probability of developing a psychological problem.

Selective serotonin reuptake inhibitors (SSRIs)—A group of medications that increase central nervous system levels of serotonin, an important neurotransmitter in the brain.

Separation anxiety disorder—An anxiety disorder that starts in childhood in which excessive anxiety is focused on separation from home or important caregivers.

Social phobia—An anxiety disorder in which a person feels excessively scared or uncomfortable in social settings or performance situations, and is fearful of embarrassment, humiliation, or social scrutiny.

Specific phobia—An anxiety disorder in which there is an excessive fear of a particular object or situation and it is avoided or causes great distress.

Symptoms—Signs of a change in a person's physical or mental health that may indicate a disease process.

Systematic desensitization—A gradual process of exposing an anxious person to objects or situations on the fear hierarchy a step at a time until anxiety is brought down to a tolerable level in the presence of these things. Starts with the least-anxiety producing things and works toward the most anxiety-producing things using coping and relaxation skills that keep anxiety low.

Temperament—Individual differences in behavioral style or emotional reactivity that are present in early life and often persist over time.

Traumatic event—A life- or health-threatening event that involves actual or possible death, injury, or threat to the physical well-being of self or others.

BIBLIOGRAPHY

Ackerman, P. T., J. E. Newton, W. B. McPherson, J. G. Jones, and R. A. Dykman. "Prevalence of Posttraumatic Stress Disorder and Other Psychiatric Diagnoses in Three Groups of Abused Children (Sexual, Physical, and Both)." *Child Abuse and Neglect* 22 (1998): 759–774.

Adams, G. B., G. A. Waas, J. S. March, and M. C. Smith. "Obsessive-Compulsive Disorder in Children and Adolescents: The Role of the School Psychologist in Identification, Assessment, and Treatment." *School Psychology Quarterly* 9(4) (1994): 274–294.

Albano, A. M., B. F. Chorpita, and D. H. Barlow. "Childhood Anxiety Disorders." *Child Psychopathology*, ed. E. J. Mash and R. A. Barkley. New York: Guilford Press, 2003: 279–329.

Albano, A.M., and P. C. Kendall. "Cognitive Behavioural Therapy for Children and Adolescents With Anxiety Disorders: Clinical Research Advances." *International Review of Psychiatry* 14 (2002): 129–134

Allen, A. J., H. L. Leonard, and S. E. Swedo. "Case Study: A New Infection-Triggered, Autoimmune Subtype of Pediatric OCD and Tourette's Syndrome." *Journal of the American Academy of Child & Adolescent Psychiatry* 34(3) (1995): 307–311.

American Psychiatric Association. *Diagnostic and Statistical Manual of Mental Disorders,* Edition 4 (DSM- IV). Washington, D.C.: American Psychiatric Association Press, 1994.

Ayers, T. S., I. N. Sandler, S. G. West, and M. W. Roosa. "A Dispositional and Situational Assessment of Children's Coping: Testing Alternative Models of Coping." *Journal of Personality* 64(4) (1996): 923–958.

Baer, L. *Getting Control.* Boston: Little, Brown, 1994.

Beidel, D. C., S. M. Turner, and T. L. Morris. "Psychopathology of Childhood Social Phobia." *Journal of the American Academy of Child and Adolescent Psychiatry* 38 (1999): 643–650.

Bergman, R. L., J. Piacentini, and J. T. McCracken. "Prevalence and Description of Selective Mutism in a School-Based Sample." *Journal of the American Academy of Child and Adolescent Psychiatry* 41 (2002): 938–946.

Biederman, J., S. V. Farane, D. R. Hirshfeld-Becker, D. Friedman, J. A. Robin, and J. F. Rosenbaum. "Patterns of Psychopathology and Dysfunction in High-Risk Children of Parents with Panic Disorder and Major Depression." *American Journal of Psychiatry* 158 (2001): 49–57.

Birmaher, B., and T. H. Ollendick. "Childhood-Onset Panic Disorder." *Phobic and Anxiety Disorders in Children and Adolescents*, ed. T. H. Ollendick and J. S. March. New York: Oxford University Press, 2004.

Bogels, S. M., and D. Zigterman. "Dysfunctional Cognitions in Children With Social Phobia, Separation Anxiety Disorder, and Generalized Anxiety Disorder." *Journal of Abnormal Child Psychology* 28 (2000): 205–211.

Cohen, J. A. "American Academy of Child and Adolescent Psychiatry Official Action: Practice Parameters for the Assessment and Treatment of Children and Adolescents With Posttraumatic Stress Disorder." *Journal of the American Academy of Child and Adolescent Psychiatry* 37(10 supplement) (1998): 4S–26S.

Costello, E. J., H. L. Egger, and A. Angold. "Developmental Epidemiology of Anxiety Disorders." *Phobic and Anxiety Disorders in Children and Adolescents*, ed. T. H. Ollendick and J. S. March. New York: Oxford University Press, 2004.

Cronk, N. J., W. S. Slutske, P. A. F. Madden, K. K. Bucholz, and A. C. Heath. "Risk for Separation Anxiety Disorder Among Girls: Parental Absence, Socioeconomic Disadvantage, and Genetic Vulnerability." *Journal of Abnormal Psychology* 113 (2004): 237–247.

Dadds, M. R., D. E. Holland, K. P. Laurens, M. Mullins, P. M. Barrett, and S. H. Spence. "Early Intervention and Prevention of Anxiety Disorders in Children: Results at Two-Year Follow-Up." *Journal of Consulting and Clinical Psychology* 67 (1999): 145–150.

Dadds, M. R., and J. H. Roth. "Family Processes in the Development of Anxiety Problems." *The Developmental Psychopathology of Anxiety*, ed. M. W. Vasey and M. R. Dadds. Oxford: Oxford University Press, 2001.

Davies, W. H., and D. J. Flannery. "Post-Traumatic Stress Disorders in Children and Adolescents Exposed to Violence: Violence Among Children and Adolescents." *Pediatric Clinics of North America* 45(2) (1998): 341–353.

Essau, C. A., J. Conradt, and F. Petermann. "Frequency of Panic Attacks and Panic Disorder in Adolescents." *Depression and Anxiety* 9 (1999): 19–26.

Foa, E. B., and R. Wilson, R. *Stop Obsessing! How to Overcome Your Obsessions and Compulsions.* New York: Bantam Doubleday Dell, 1991.

Geller, D.A., J. Biederman, S. E. Stewart, B. Mullin, A. Martin, T. Spencer, and S. V. Faraone. "Which SSRI? A Meta-Analysis of Pharmacotherapy Trials in Pediatric Obsessive-Compulsive Disorder." *American Journal of Psychiatry* 160 (2003): 1919–1928.

Giaconia, R. M., H. Z. Reinherz, A. B. Silverman, B. Pakiz, A. K. Frost, and E. Cohen. "Traumas and Posttraumatic Stress Disorder in a Community Population of Older Adolescents." *Journal of the American Academy of Child and Adolescent Psychiatry* 34 (1995): 1369–1380.

Ginsburg, G. S., and J. T. Walkup. "Specific Phobia." *Phobic and Anxiety Disorders in Children and Adolescents*, ed. T. H. Ollendick and J. S. March. New York: Oxford University Press, 2004.

Hesser, T. S. *Kissing Doorknobs.* New York: Delacorte Press, 1998.

Ialongo, N., G. Edelsohn, L. Werthamer-Larsson, L. Crockett, and S. Kellam, "The Significance of Self-Reported Anxious Symptoms in First Grade Children: Prediction to Anxious Symptoms and Adaptive Functioning in Fifth Grade." *Journal of Child Psychology and Psychiatry* 36 (1995): 427–437

Kagan, J., and N. Snidman. "Early Childhood Predictors of Adult Anxiety Disorders." *Biological Psychiatry* 46 (1999): 1536–1541.

Kearney, C. A., A. M. Albano, A. R. Eisen, W. D. Allan, and D. H. Barlow. "The Phenomenology of Panic Disorder in Youngsters: An Empirical Study of a Clinical Sample." *Journal of Anxiety Disorders* 11 (1997): 49–63.

Kendall, P. C. *Coping Cat Workbook*. Ardmore, PA: Workbook Publishing, 1992.

Kendall, P. C., S. Pimentel, M. A. Rynn, A. Angelosante, and A. Webb. "Generalized Anxiety Disorder." *Phobic and Anxiety Disorders in Children and Adolescents*, ed. T. H. Ollendick and J. S. March. New York: Oxford University Press, 2004.

King, N. J., P. Muris, and T. H. Ollendick. "Specific Phobia." *Anxiety Disorders in Children and Adolescents*, 2nd ed., ed. T. L. Morris and J. S. March. New York: Guilford Press, 2004.

Levin, M., S. Ashmore-Callahan, P. Kendall, and M. Ichii M (1996). "Treatment of Separation Anxiety Disorder." *Cognitive Therapy with Children and Adolescents*, ed. M. Reinecke, F. Dattilio, and A. Freeman. New York: Guilford Press, 1996.

March, J. S., H. L. Leonard, and S. E. Swedo. "Anxiety Disorders in Children and Adolescents." *Obsessive-Compulsive Disorder*. New York: Guilford Press, 1995.

March, J., and K. Mulle. *How I Ran OCD Off My Land: A Guide to Cognitive-Behavioral Psychotherapy for Children and Adolescents with Obsessive-Compulsive Disorder*. New York: Guilford Press, 1998.

Masi, G., M. Mucci, L. Favilla, R. Romano, and P. Poli. "Symptomatology and Comorbidity of Generalized Anxiety Disorder in Children and Adolescents." *Comprehensive Psychiatry* 40 (1999): 210–215.

McCloskey, L. A., and M. Walker. "Posttraumatic Stress in Children Exposed to Family Violence and Single-Event Trauma." *Journal of the American Academy of Child and Adolescent Psychiatry* 26(5) (2000): 764–769.

McKnight, C. D., S. N. Compton, and J. S. March. "Posttraumatic Stress Disorder." *Anxiety Disorders in Children and Adolescents*, 2nd ed., ed. T. L. Morris and J. S. March. New York: Guilford Press, 2004.

Mendels, J. "Clinical Drug Appraisal: Sertraline." *Drug Therapy* 22 (1992): 37–48.

Murphy, T. K., W. K. Goodman, M. W. Fudge, M. W., et al. "Beta Lymphocyte Antigen D8/17: A Peripheral Marker for Childhood-Onset Obsessive Compulsive Disorder and Tourette's Syndrome." *American Journal of Psychiatry* 154 (1997): 402–407.

Ollendick, T. H. "Panic Disorder in Children and Adolescents: New Developments, New Directions." *Journal of Clinical Child Psychology* 27 (1998): 234–245.

Ollendick T. H., and J. March. "Integrated Psychosocial and Pharmacological Treatment." *Phobic and Anxiety Disorders in Children and Adolescents*, ed. T. H. Ollendick and J. S. March. New York: Oxford University Press, 2004.

Perrin, S., P. Smith, and W. Yule. "Practitioner Review: The Assessment and Treatment of Post-Traumatic Stress Disorder in Children and Adolescents." *Journal Child Psychology & Psychiatry* 41(3) (2000): 277–289.

Perry, B. D., and I. Azad. "Posttraumatic Stress Disorders in Children and Adolescents." *Current Opinion in Pediatrics* 11(4) (1999): 310–320.

Pine, D. S., P. Cohen, D. Gurley, J. Brook, and Y. Ma "The Risk for Early-Adulthood Anxiety and Depressive Disorders in Adolescents with Anxiety and Depressive Disorders." *Archives of General Psychiatry* 55 (1998): 56–64.

Preskorn, S. H. "Pharmacokinetics of Psychiatric Agents: Why and How They are Relevant to Treatment." *Journal of Clinical Psychiatry* 54 (suppl) (1993): 3–12.

Pynoos, R. S. "Grief and Trauma in Children and Adolescents." *Bereavement Care* 2 (1992): 2–10.

Pynoos, R., and K. Nader. "Prevention of Psychiatric Morbidity in Children and Disaster." *Disaster Information: A Resource Kit,* ed. R. S. Pynoos and K. Nader. Washington, DC: American Academy of Child and Adolescent Psychiatry Press, 1990.

Silverman W., and A. M. Albano. *Manual for the Anxiety Disorders Interview Schedule for DSM-IV: Child and Parent Versions*. San Antonio, TX: Psychological Corporation, 1996.

Spence, S. H. "Prevention Strategies." *The Developmental Psychopathology of Anxiety*, ed. M. W. Vasey and M. R. Dadds. Oxford: Oxford University Press, 2001.

Steketee, G., and K. White. *When Once Is Not Enough; Help for Obsessive-Compulsives*. Oakland, CA: Harbinger Publications, 1990.

Swedo, S. E. (1994). "Sydenham's Chorea: A Model for Childhood Autoimmune Disorders." *Journal of the American Medical Association*: 272 (1994): 1788–1791.

Swedo, S. E., H. L. Leonard, B. Mittleman, et al. (1997). "Identification of Children with Pediatric Autoimmune Neuropsychiatric Disorders Associated with Streptococcal Infections by a Marker Associated with Rheumatic Fever." *American Journal of Psychiatry* 154 (1997): 110–112.

Terr, L. C. "Childhood Traumas: An Outline and Overview." *American Journal of Psychiatry* 148 (1991): 10–20.

Woodward, L. J., and D. M. Fergusson. "Life Course Outcomes of Young People with Anxiety Disorders in Adolescence." *Journal of the American Academy of Child and Adolescent Psychiatry* 40 (2001): 1086–1093.

FURTHER READING

Baer, L. *Getting Control.* Boston: Little, Brown, 1991.

Chansky, T. E. *Freeing Your Child from Obsessive-Compulsive Disorder.* New York: Three Rivers Press, 2000.

Dornbush, M. P., and S. K. Pruitt. *Teaching the Tiger.* Duarte, CA: Hope Press, 1995.

Foa, E. B., and R. Wilson. *Stop Obsessing! How to Overcome Your Obsessions and Compulsions.* New York: Bantam Doubleday, 1991.

Manassis, K. *Keys to Parenting Your Anxious Child.* New York: Barron's Educational Series, Inc., 1996.

Rapee, R., S. Spence, V. Cobham, and A. Wignall. *Helping Your Anxious Child.* Oakland, CA: New Harbinger Publications, Inc., 2000.

American Academy of Child and Adolescent Psychiatry

www.aacap.org

Association for Behavioral and Cognitive Therapies
(formerly Association for the Advancement of Behavioral Therapy)

www.aabt.org

National Alliance on Mental Illness (NAMI)

www.nami.org

National Institute of Mental Health

www.nimh.nih.gov

National OC Foundation, Inc.

www.ocfoundation.org

Obsessive-Compulsive Foundation of Metropolitan Chicago

www.ocfchicago.org

Selective Mutism Foundation, Inc.

www.selectivemutismfoundation.org

Selective Mutism Group-Childhood Anxiety Network

www.selectivemutism.org

Trichotillomania Learning Center

www.trich.org

INDEX

Academic functioning, 12
    and GAD, 4, 10, 21, 23, 25, 29, 31
    interference with, 1, 3–4, 10, 16, 21, 39, 44, 46, 52, 75, 95
    and OCD, 75, 81
    and panic attacks, 66
    poor concentration, 4, 23, 92, 95, 100
    and PTSD, 92, 95, 100
    and SAD, 1–4, 35, 39
    and social phobia, 44, 46
    and specific phobia, 52
Acute stress disorder, 93
ADHD. *See* Attention-deficit/hyperactivity disorder
ADIS-C. *See* Anxiety Disorders Interview Schedule–Child Version
Agoraphobia
    causes, 40
    and children, 2
    defined, 3, 69
    statistics, 3
Alprazolam (Xanax®), 19
Anafranil®. *See* Clomipramine
Antidepressants
    and anxiety disorders, 17–19, 31, 40
    and panic disorders, 71
    and PTSD, 104
    and social phobia, 51
    and specific phobia, 62
    and suicidal thoughts, 18
    types, 17–19
Antipsychotic medications, 104
Anxiety disorders
    and co-occurring disorders, 9, 11, 17–19, 28, 31, 36, 48–50, 52, 55, 63–64, 95–96, 99
    development of, 1–7
    future, 105
    impact on functioning, 1–4
    risk and protective factors, 3–7
    statistics, 3
    versus normal fears, 1–3, 8, 32, 52, 76
Anxiety Disorders Interview Schedule–Child Version (ADIS-C), 11
Asthma, 8
Ativan®. *See* Lorazepam
Attention-deficit/hyperactivity disorder (ADHD)
    and anxiety disorders, 9, 11, 17–18, 101

Avoidant coping, 6
    and OCD, 86
    and panic disorders, 64–65, 69–70
    and PTSD, 89, 103–104
    and SAD, 36, 39
    and social phobia, 41–44, 46, 48–49
    and specific phobias, 53, 56

Behavioral inhibition
    caution, 6
    emotional restraint, 6
    shyness, 6
Benzodiazepines
    action, 19
    dependence and side effects, 19
    and panic disorders, 71
    research on, 19
    and specific phobia, 62
    treatment, 19
Bipolar disorder, 17
BuSpar®. *See* Buspirone
Buspirone (BuSpar®), 19

Caffeine, 8
CBT. *See* Cognitive behavioral therapy
Celexa®. *See* Citalopram hydrobromide
Characteristics, GAD
    chronic and uncontrollable worry, 2, 21, 23, 29–30, 55, 64
    perfectionist worries, 4, 10, 21, 23, 28–30
    performance fears, 4, 20–21, 27, 31
    physical illnesses, 21, 23–24, 28
    self-doubt, 10, 28
Characteristics, OCD
    compulsive behaviors, 72–75, 77–78, 80
    excessive worrying, 79
    obsessive images, 72–73, 75–77
    repeated questions, 77–78
    and stress, 72, 83
Characteristics, Panic disorder
    avoidance of situations, 64–65, 69–70
    fear of being ill and losing control, 67–68, 69
    impending doom, 63
    isolation, 69
    repeated anxiety attacks without trigger, 2, 63–65, 67, 70
    worries of panic attacks, 67, 69–70
Characteristics, PTSD
    emotional impacts and, 90–92, 95–96, 102–103

flushed face, 43, 47
freezing or shrinking, 44
irritability, 44
negative thoughts, 43
shaky hands, 43, 47
shyness, 44
stomachaches, 46, 52, 69
Symptoms, Specific phobia
crying, 55
difficulty breathing, 57
freezing or shrinking, 55
heart racing, 52, 57
irritability, 55
stomachaches, 52
sweating, 57
Systematic desensitization, 14
and PSTD, 103
and specific phobia, 61–62

TCAs. *See* Tricyclic antidepressants
Thyroid disease, 8, 21
Tourette's syndrome, 84
Treatment, Anxiety disorders, 13–19
combination, 17
and education, 13
and evaluation, 9–10, 12, 17, 105
family interventions, 13–16
goals, 6–7
medications, 13, 17–19
parent-child interventions, 15–16
psychotherapy, 6, 13–15, 17
school interventions, 13–14, 16
Treatment, GAD
combination, 26
and evaluation, 25–29
family interventions, 26
medications, 25–26, 28, 31
parent-child interventions, 26, 30
psychotherapy, 25–26, 28, 30
school interventions, 31
Treatment, OCD
combination, 87, 96, 101
and education, 79, 81, 85
family interventions, 78–80, 88
medications, 81, 83, 85, 87
parent-child interventions, 80, 88
psychotherapy, 78–81, 85–87

school interventions, 81–82
support groups, 87
Treatment, Panic disorders
and education, 71, 79, 81, 85
medications, 64, 71
parent-child interventions, 63–65
psychotherapy, 65, 71
Treatment, PTSD
combination, 96, 101
family interventions, 97–98, 102–103
medications, 95–96, 99, 102–104
psychotherapy, 96–98, 101, 103–104
support groups, 102–103
Treatment, SAD
and education, 37, 59–60, 71, 79, 81, 85
and evaluation, 37
family interventions, 37, 40
goals, 40
medications, 40
parent-child interventions, 40
psychotherapy, 37,
school interventions, 37, 40
Treatment, Social phobia
family interventions, 42, 46
goals, 42–43, 45
medications, 42, 49, 51
parent-child interventions, 52–62
psychotherapy, 42, 46, 49, 51
school interventions, 42, 46
Treatment, Specific phobia
and education, 59–60
and evaluation, 60
medications, 57, 60–61
parent-child interventions, 15–16, 26, 30, 40, 42, 46–65, 80, 88
psychotherapy, 57–61
Tricyclic antidepressants (TCAs)
and OCD, 87
side effects, 18, 87

Venlafaxine (Effexor®), 18

Xanax®. *See* Alprazolam

Zoloft®. *See* Sertraline

PICTURE CREDITS

Anafranil is a registered trademark of Mallinckrodt Inc.; Ativan is a registered trademark of Wyeth Laboratories, Inc.; BuSpar is a registered trademark of Bristol-Myers Squibb Company; Celexa is a registered trademark of Forest Pharmaceuticals; Effexor is a registered trademark of Wyeth Pharmaceuticals; Klonopin is a registered trademark of Hoffman-La Roche Inc.; Lexapro is a registered trademark of Forest Laboratories; Luvox is a registered trademark of Solvay Pharmaceuticals, Inc.; Paxil is a registered trademark of GlaxoSmithKline; Prozac is a registered trademark of Eli Lilly and Company; Xanax is a registered trademark of Pfizer Inc.; Zoloft is a registered trademark of Pfizer Inc.

Sucheta Connolly, MD, is a child and adolescent psychiatrist, associate professor of clinical psychiatry, and director of the Pediatric Stress and Anxiety Disorders Clinic at University of Illinois at Chicago (UIC). Dr. Connolly graduated from Washington University Medical School in St. Louis and completed her residency in general psychiatry at UIC and her fellowship in child and adolescent psychiatry at University of Chicago. Dr. Connolly provides evaluation, treatment, training, and school consultation in childhood anxiety disorders. Her research interests include selective mutism and risk and protective factors in childhood anxiety.

David Simpson, MSSA, LCSW, is a licensed clinical social worker who is the clinic and research coordinator for the Pediatric Stress and Anxiety Disorders Clinic at the University of Illinois at Chicago (UIC). Mr. Simpson graduated from the Mandel School of Applied Social Sciences at Case Western Reserve University with a master of science in social administration. In addition to his administrative responsibilities, he performs therapy with children, adolescents, their families, and adults who have anxiety disorders. Recently, Mr. Simpson began a PhD in social work and will conduct research on risk and protective factors in childhood anxiety.

Cynthia Petty MS, APRN, BC, is a certified advanced practice nurse who specializes in treating OCD and other anxiety disorders in children and adolescents. She received her bachelor's degree in nursing and her master of science degrees from the University of Illinois at Chicago. Ms. Petty is certified by the American Nurses Credentialing Center as a clinical specialist in child and adolescent psychiatric and mental health nursing. She also is certified by the Behavior Institute as a provider of cognitive-behavioral therapy. She has worked at the University of Illinois at Chicago in the OCD and Tic Disorders Clinic for two years and in the Pediatric Stress & Anxiety Disorder Clinic for five years providing individual therapy and medication management.